The Kitching Whittaker Enneagram Adventure

Copyright © Jennie Kitching and Brit Whittaker 2017
The rights of Jennie Kitching and Brit Whittaker to be identified as the authors of this work has been asserted by them in accordance with the Copyright, Designs and Patents Act, 1988. All rights reserved. Without limiting the rights under copyrights above, no part of this publication may be reproduced, stored in, or introduced into a retrieval system, or transmitted, in any form or by any means (electronic, mechanical, photocopying, recording, or otherwise), without the express prior written permission of the copyright owners aforementioned.

By purchasing this book you agree that you have read and understand that all information is subject to the reader's interpretation. The authors will not be held accountable for any interpretations or decisions made by recipients based on information provided herein.

This information is for education and entertainment purposes only. All information and/or advice given to you herein should not take the place of any medical, legal or financial advice given to you by any qualified professional. Any names or characters within this book are the product of the author's imagination and any resemblance to real persons, living or dead is completely coincidental.

For more information contact info@hiprocom.com.

Author Biography

Jennie Kitching AdvDipH ADPR SQHP –

Head teacher of The Advanced Diploma in Hypnosis and A Master Hypnotist and counselor since 2003. Since that time she has become a certified teacher of a variety of differing methodologies in the corporate and private sector. Jennie is also an after dinner speaker who presents with humor and enthusiasm drawing on an extensive knowledge base. Together with partner and fellow contributing author, Brit KS Whittaker, she writes, teaches and delivers this knowledge to international audiences. Visit Hiprocom.com to discover more or for engagements and bookings contact info@hiprocom.com.

How to use this book	10
Preface: The Map	12
Introduction: True Fact or a Lesson for the Kiddies?	14
Other People	*16*
Your Changing Self	*16*
Enneagram Background History	*17*
Keeping the Secret	*17*
Why Learn Enneagram?	*19*
Are you ready for your Enneagram Adventure?	21
Your Enneagram Adventure	22
The Invitation	*22*
Welcome Adventure Seekers!	96
The Right One	100
The Helpful One	*102*
The Striving for Success One	*104*
The I'm the Only One	*106*
The Thoughtful One	*108*
The Safe One	*110*
The Fun One	*112*
The War One	*114*
The Peace One	*116*
The imprint of your soul	118
Going Deeper: The Beginnings of Distrust and Separation	*120*
Separation	120
Distrust	121
Reactions to Separation	123
Delusions	124
Important Folks and Written Records	125
The Devil Made Me Do It!	129
Enneagram and the Kabbalah	*129*
Your Evolving, Revolving, Dissolving Self	133
Your Evolving Self	*134*
Your Revolving Self	*135*
Your Dissolving Self	*136*
Unwanted Behaviour	*137*
We are not our Behaviours	*137*

- *Everyone is the same? Know Thyself* 138
- *It's Just Me!* 138
- *You are a Number!* 139
- *Enlightenment* 139
- *Finding Direction* 140
- *Mood Swings* 141

Your Typing Tunnel 142
- *Verifying Your Number Type* 142

1. Find Your Triad 143
- *The Gut* 143
- *The Head* 145
- *The Heart* 146
- *DECISION TIME: WHICH TRIAD ARE YOU?* 147

2. Getting Stuck on Fixations 149
- *Fixate On Your Poisons and Prisons* 150
- *DECISION TIME: WHAT IS YOUR FIXATION?* 152

3. Find Your Trap 154
- *Lack and Disconnection with Source* 154
- *The Holy Ideas* 154
- *I am a Perfectionist* 156
- *I love Freedom* 156
- *I am Efficient* 156
- *I am Authentic* 157
- *I am a keen Observer* 157
- *I like my Security* 157
- *I am an Idealist* 157
- *I want Justice* 158
- *I am a Seeker* 158
- *DECISION TIME: WHAT IS YOUR TRAP?* 158

4. Find Your Sin 160
- Anger 161
- Pride 161
- Deceit 162
- Envy 162
- Avarice 162
- Fear 163
- Gluttony 163

- Excess 163
- Laziness 164
- *DECISION TIME: WHAT IS YOUR SIN?* *164*
- **5. Find Your Wound** **166**
  - Wound of Being Evil or Corrupt 167
  - Wound of Being Unloved or Unwanted 168
  - Wound of Being Worthless or Without Value 169
  - Wound of Being Special 170
  - Wound of Being Incapable or Incompetent 172
  - Wound of Being Without Support or Guidance 174
  - Wound of Being Trapped or In Pain 175
  - Wound of Being Hurt or Controlled 177
  - Wound of Separation and Loss 178
  - *DECISION TIME: WHAT IS YOUR WOUND?* *180*
- **6. Harmonic Patterns : How We Handle Our Frustrations** **181**
  - Three ways we handle our frustrations: 181
  - *Competency* *182*
    - How to handle frustration with competency 182
  - *Positive Outlook* *185*
    - How to handle frustration with positive outlook 186
  - *Reactive* *189*
    - How to handle frustration with reactivity 189
  - *DECISION TIME: HOW DO YOU HANDLE FRUSTRATION?* *192*
- **7. Hornevian Type : How We Solve Conflict** **193**
  - *Compliance* *194*
    - How to solve conflict with compliance 195
      - The Right Compliance 195
      - The Helpful Compliance 196
      - The Safe Compliance 197
  - *Withdraw* *198*
    - How to solve conflict by withdrawing 200
      - Withdraw to Inner Emotional Realm 200
      - Withdraw to The Mental Realm 201
      - Withdraw by Invisibility Cloaking 202
  - *Assertive* *203*
    - How to solve conflict by asserting yourself 204
      - Assertion of Entitlement 204

- Assertion of Desire 206
- Assertion of Strength 207
- *DECISION TIME: HOW DO YOU SOLVE CONFLICT? 210*

8. Focus of Attention – Where Our Energy Naturally Gravitates To 211
- *External or Internal 211*
- *External 212*
- *Internal 214*
- *DECISION TIME: WHERE IS YOUR FOCUS OF ATTENTION? 215*

9. Find Your Virtue 217
- *Serenity 218*
- *Humility 218*
- *Truthfulness 218*
- *Equanimity 219*
- *Detachment 219*
- *Courage 219*
- *Sobriety 220*
- *Innocence 220*
- *Right Action 220*
- *DECISION TIME: SO WHAT IS YOUR VIRTUE? 221*

10. Find Your Fear 222
- *The fear of being evil or corrupt 222*
- *The fear of being unloved or unwanted by others 224*
- *The fear of being worthless 225*
- *The fear of not being special 226*
- *The fear of being useless or incapable. 227*
- *The fear of being without support or guidance. 228*
- *The fear of being restricted and in pain 230*
- *The fear of being hurt or controlled by others 231*
- *The fear of separation and loss 232*
- *DECISION TIME: WHAT IS YOUR FEAR? 234*

YOUR DECISION = YOUR NUMBER! 235
- *ANSWER: DECISION TIME: WHICH TRIAD ARE YOU? 235*
- *ANSWER: DECISION TIME: WHAT IS YOUR FIXATION? 236*
- *ANSWER: DECISION TIME: WHAT IS YOUR TRAP? 236*
- *ANSWER: DECISION TIME: WHAT IS YOUR SIN? 237*

ANSWER: DECISION TIME: WHAT IS YOUR WOUND? *238*
ANSWER: DECISION TIME: HOW DO YOU HANDLE FRUSTRATION? *239*
ANSWER: DECISION TIME: HOW DO YOU SOLVE CONFLICT? *239*
ANSWER: DECISION TIME: WHERE IS YOUR FOCUS OF ATTENTION? *240*
ANSWER: DECISION TIME: SO WHAT IS YOUR VIRTUE? .. *241*
ANSWER: DECISION TIME: WHAT IS YOUR FEAR? *242*
The Antidotes to Illusions and Delusions *244*
Practical Advice *245*
   It's Alright for YOU! 246
The Antidote to Your Trap: **249**
   The Antidote to Perfection 249
   The Antidote to Freedom 250
   The Antidote to Efficiency 250
   The Antidote to Authenticity 251
   The Antidote to Observation 251
   The Antidote to Security 252
   The Antidote to Idealism 252
   The Antidote to Justice 253
   The Antidote to Indolence 253
   WHAT IS YOUR ANTIDOTE? *254*
YOUR NUMBER TYPE REVEALED 256
Time to Be No.1 257
It's Time to Help You No.2s 259
Time to Be Image Free for No.3s 261
Time to Be More for All the 4s 263
Time to Thrive For No.5s 265
Time for The Unrestrictive No.6s 267
Time to Get Out Of Heaven, No.7s 269
No Time To Infuriate the No.8s 271
Time to Re-Align the No.9s 273
Exclusive to Kitching Whittaker Enneagram 275
   The Hidden Secret at Your Core & The Way Forward *275*
The Way Forward for 1s 276
The Way Forward for 2s 278

The Way Forward for 3s 280
The Way Forward for 4s 282
The Way Forward for 5s 284
The Way Forward for 6s 286
The Way Forward for 7s 289
The Way Forward for 8s 291
The Way Forward for 9s 293
   Fame and Fortune Typed! -Donald Trump 295
   Countries of the World Typed! 297
   Coming Soon! BOOK 2 of The Kitching Whittaker
   Enneagram Adventure 299
   Tell us about your issue 299
Thank you for reading 300

How to use this book

Your Enneagram Adventure begins here.

The Kitching Whittaker Enneagram Adventure is comprised of three main parts.

Part One: The Adventure
This is an interactive action adventure fictional tale. You are asked at each stage of the journey to make a decision. Your decision determines the next section of the story for you, culminating in the chapter 'What Are You Like?' which offers your number type based on your own personal adventure choices.

Part Two: Your Typing Tunnel
There are Ten Sections within the Tunnel. At the end of each section you make a note of your preferred choice and then arrive at the chapter 'Your Decision = Your Type'. Your choices will determine your Triad, your Fixation, your Trap, your Sin, your Wound, your Harmonic Pattern, (how you handle frustration), your Hornevian Type (how you deal with conflict), your Focus of attention, your Virtue and your Fear.

Part Three: Exclusive to Kitching Whittaker Enneagram - The Hidden Secret at Your Core & The Way Forward

Having determined your number type, either from The Adventure, Your Typing Tunnel or both, you then get access the illnesses or issues that your type is predisposed to and you will also discover the secret at the core of your personality! So, let's begin your adventure.

Preface: The Map

Buried deep in an underground cave, lost in the magic of time, lies *a map of ancient origin that holds the secrets to life,* the universe and everything.

This map depicts the workings of hidden powerful forces acting upon Human Beings to which each individual must succumb. These forces are so imperceptibly woven deep into each human psyche that a person would know them as part of their 'true self' and defend them as part of their very nature; their very essence.

As mankind created pairings and then families, then workgroups and towns and cities, so these aspects and divisions of personality would become more and more apparent; the differences between human beings would surface and cause conflict.

In each conflict, each human would inevitably think that they were right to behave and think as they do, forming societies and clandestine groups, strengthening their viewpoint and wondering why everyone else could not be like them. Disagreement led to ostracising, condemnation and fighting in the name of what is right. These energies turned man against his brother until man might live no more.

The map also revealed pathways to overcoming these traits; to rise above each negative force acting upon each personality, to engage with the positive polar opposite of each condition. Though it would take an awareness, a profound willingness to rise above the person's very nature to wonder if there was a better way. It would take experimentation, a brave commitment to put one's faith in a higher ideal, to rise above disagreement with others and within the self. It would take a recognition that hurting each other meant hurting the self and it would take a deep desire for unity and to feel and be better and to strive for improvement.

This voyage through the map would begin with acknowledging and rising above the negative ego.

The negative ego learnt quickly and began to fight back.

Introduction: True Fact or a Lesson for the Kiddies?

Mankind has been seeking since, forever, to improve his condition; to move away from pain and towards pleasure.

In fulfilling personal needs and pursuing measures of pleasure in one form or another, we found fear and lack: fear that there was not enough and lack that someone else would acquire it all first.

It is the form of this pleasure and fulfilment of personal needs that drive our personality. We all have one. We all have an ego. Accepting this is crucial. Ego is fine. Negative Ego is the baddie.

Your Negative Ego disguises itself as your friend and it is not. It causes you to dissolve into floods of tears, to just 'switch off' and disconnect with everyone, to throw your teddy in the corner (or whatever is close to hand) or to plan your vengeance for some time in the future that may never come, though the thoughts keep us warm at night as we complain the world and its people are not to our liking.

I'm not talking of true emotion; energy in motion propelling us towards our desires and away from undesirable stuff is a good thing. I am talking about the overwhelming panic ridden state of trying at all costs to protect oneself, using various behaviours, and being in the seemingly hopeless grip of some force compelling us towards a well of despair of one form or another.

So, this ancient system (yes, it is ancient and has been corrupted, converted, cannibalised into many forms, including the 7 Deadly Sins by the way) is a map.

You need a map.

No one ever told me about this map. I think if it were included in the National Curriculum then many of our adolescent frustrations and our adult yearnings, frustrations and regrets would be far easier to handle.

Here we are then. *Your guide to Life, The Universe and Everything.* Well, your guide to you and your personality in any case PLUS how to get along with everyone else who happens to be sharing the planet with you.

Other People

You may have come to this work to understand yourself and that is highly commendable; or you may have come to this to understand others, which is equally laudable. The interesting thing is that whether you begin looking outward or inward, this will benefit your whole life. Did I say your whole life? Well yes I meant it. *Your whole life will improve with this knowledge.* Yes it will.

Your Changing Self

Everything is energy and everything is in a constant state of flux. Change is the only constant in life and yet we often fight to attempt to prevent it and preserve the status quo.

Your environment, behaviour, skills and abilities, beliefs and values and even your identity change as we go through life and are affected as we respond to the challenges presented.

Some of us notice the repeating patterns, 'why does this ALWAYS happen to me!'.

We may move job, country, change our partner, lose touch with family or have someone close to us die.

However, as our awareness increases, we may find the same attributes appearing in our new partner; we may find ourselves working with the very personality we tried to escape in our old job.

Yes, everything is energy and everything has its pattern of creation, even you.

Enneagram Background History

Like the Kabbalah, the Enneagram was an oral tradition, passed on by word of mouth only to those capable of understanding its message. Nowadays, with the internet revolution, nothing can be hidden any more.

Keeping the Secret

Teachers are of the opinion that the treasures will remain hidden to those who do not have the capacity or willingness to understand this map, so therefore all is well.

Just like the Kabbalah, one can perceive the image as a flat one dimensional diagram, though when one truly knows its many dimensions, the Kabbalah becomes a four dimensional mandala full of mystery and energy, a swirling living pulsating mass of potential. Thus it also is with the Enneagram.

For some, the Enneagram will only ever be a party trick, or a corporate methodology of attempting to harness the human resource of a workforce.

For others, like you, it can be so very much more. It can *reveal secrets currently beyond comprehension* and can provide insight into understanding and contemplation of the entire human condition.

Oh yes, it can also help you get on so much better with your loved ones and explain why the people you love are often the very ones who test your mettle and throw you headlong into evolving … AND dissolving! Oh, didn't I mention the dissolving bit?

Why Learn Enneagram?

Ever wondered why you passionately want something or someone: what drives you? We can peel back the layers to reveal and discover our personality drive.

Ever truly wondered what you could actually do to 'rise above the ego'? We can stop being blindly driven by it.

Ever wanted to really understand what all this anxiety and fear was all about and why not everyone else shared yours? We can end the uncertainty, fear, and anxiety of being so driven by energies and forces we do not yet understand.

Ever really wanted to be back in control? We can take charge and start driving our own lives with confidence and resolve.

Knowing this ancient matrix, we can celebrate being victorious at life and being victorious at living our destiny.

Knowing this, we can be triumphant with a life enriched with loving and caring and rich with wonder and mystery; we can be happy.

Working with an ancient matrix called Enneagram.

Yes, we can find the drive of personality and we can find more of ourselves.

We can unravel the circuitry of our Subconscious Mind, restructuring it.

We can begin by revealing the secrets of our Unconscious Self, we can forge forward with strength and insight. We can work with the matrix of Enneagram as no one has done before.

Noting how we 'dissolve' and 'evolve' our emphasis is upon our elevation and integration. With this focus and emphasis, we guide you into many mysteries that call for your understanding.

We lift the veils of perception and of resistance so that we might unlock the sheer and beautiful forces of Enneagram with an overflowing of wonder and celebration. Once unlocked, we can utilise those otherwise untapped forces and flows as our resources for the present and our most favourable future.

THAT is why *learning the Kitching Whittaker Enneagram is so important!*

Are you ready for your Enneagram Adventure?

We have devised a novel and interesting, never seen before, method of discovering what Enneagram number you are.

This is your Adventure. It is *an interactive fictional tale specially written for you*.

Along the way you will be asked to choose your next step - answer as honestly as you can and don't spend too much time deliberating. Later, it may be fun to ask your nearest and dearest if they agree with your answer, or to get them to do it too!

It begins.

Your Enneagram Adventure

SECTION 1

The Invitation

You receive an invitation in the post. You are cordially invited to the Infinity Mansion to attend a very special dinner.

You are promised a night of intrigue and discovery. The invitation is far too intriguing to ignore and so you decide to go.

The night arrives and you make your way to the Infinity Mansion. At the front door you ring the buzzer which is answered by a surly old butler who greets you with, Good evening my name is Jeeves. Welcome may I take your coat?

You take the opportunity to ask Jeeves, as you pass him your coat,

DECISION TIME!

Chose one of the options listed below and click on the link.

A What is this all about? **Go to Section2, PAGE 28**

OR:

B Are there many coming tonight? **Go to Section3, PAGE 25**

OR:

C You simply follow Jeeves as he leads you into the dining room. **Go to Section4, PAGE 26**

SECTION 2

Jeeves says I am afraid I don't know, I was just hired for this evening's dinner and on arrival I was given a book of instructions.

Jeeves then leads you to the dining room. **Go to Section4, PAGE 26**

SECTION 3

Jeeves says that he was only hired today for this one off job and he has no idea how many people are coming. Jeeves then leads you to the dining room.
Go to Section4, PAGE 26

SECTION 4

You enter the dining room with Jeeves. The dining room is a large room.

Down one side there is a buffet and in the middle of the room there are many small tables laid out with plates and silver knives and forks, candelabras etc.

There are a handful of people milling about the buffet. Suddenly, all of the windows and the doors lock shut. A voice can be heard over an intercom system, saying welcome to the Infinity Mansion.

This mansion I have created as a deadly puzzle. If you do not escape by midnight, you will die.

There are several individuals around that are there to provide the help you need to get to the truth and escape with your life. You have three hours remaining. Good luck.

Here are the five characters specifically placed in order to help you. Who do you approach. Do you approach:

DECISION TIME!

A Gerard

The man dressed in an Armani suit with a gold Rolex watch. He seems very organised and efficient, which inspires confidence. **Go to Section5, PAGE 30**

OR:

B Florence
The young woman with a sore foot. She has mousey unkempt hair, looking somewhat anxious. She is sitting in a chair with her shoe off, rubbing her foot. She seems to be in pain. **Go to Section6, PAGE 31**

OR:

C Ronald
The geeky looking young man with instruction books. He is sitting at a table wearing a smart white shirt with a starched collar. He has a number of books around him. These are carefully arranged books. **Go to Section7, PAGE 32**

OR:

D Merlin the Second
The Rastafarian man who is middle aged, sitting back in his chair. He is wearing tie-dyed coloured clothing. He seems very relaxed and is smiling broadly. **Go to Section8, PAGE 33**

OR:

E Gladys
The tall muscular Nurse who seems very fit and able. She looks about six foot tall and is wearing a starched nurse's uniform.   **Go to Section9, PAGE 34**

OR:

Don't approach anyone and select your own table. There are three tables to choose from. Choose your table.

F The Drinks Table
Choose The Drinks Table near the entrance which gives you a commanding view of the entire room. There is no chair but you are happy to stand. People come up occasionally to fix themselves a drink and this gives you an opportunity to engage them in conversation and find out a little about them. You can see all the comings and goings and who is talking to who. **Go to Section10, PAGE 35**

OR:

G The Reading Table
Choose The Reading Table on the left side of the room alongside the bookcase. There is a high backed wooden chair next to the table. On the wall next to this table there is a map dated 1853 that no one else has noticed. It may not be entirely up to date though gives you some knowledge of the overall layout and entrances and exits. **Go to Section14, PAGE 43**

OR:

H The Coffee Table
Choose The Coffee Table. There is a small coffee table tucked away at the back of the room with a compact armchair by the side of it. It is in a quiet corner so no one can see you though you get a general idea of what is going on in the room. **Go to Section15, PAGE 44**

SECTION 5

Gerard is standing by the buffet and you introduce yourself and he shakes your hand firmly saying, my name is Gerard and I am thrilled to meet you. I think you would make a great addition to my team. I was here a few years' ago as the Count's Financial Adviser. I know a little bit about the layout and I also know that whoever wins this will be rewarded handsomely and let me tell you now, WE are going to be the winners!

DECISION TIME!

A He seems driven and enthusiastic and your sort of person. You think he is the winning choice so you stick with him. **Go to Section16, PAGE 45**

OR:

B You decide to choose someone else. **Go to Section11, PAGE 37**

SECTION 6

Florence says:

"I was called in for a few months a while ago as a horticultural and wildfowl consultant for the grounds and no one knows these gardens better than me, so I might be able to get us out of here. However, I have hurt my foot somehow, I'm a bit accident prone they tell me! So, I may need just a bit of help walking."

DECISION TIME!

Do you:

A Feel that this is a very genuine person though she will need some help to get through which you are happy to do. **Go to Section21, PAGE 53**

OR:

B You decide to choose someone else. **Go to Section11, PAGE 37**

SECTION 7

Ronald greets you warmly with a nod of the head and beckons you to a chair.

He says:
"On a bookshelf on the way in I found this really interesting old book. It is the history of the Infinity Manor and lo and behold the Instruction Guide to the Manor too! Jeeves the butler said it was perfectly okay for me to have them. I'm thrilled!

"Everything you need to know about this place is all here, in chronological order. There is a fabulous index at the back too, with everything cross referenced so I find any information at a glance. I think that if we follow these two guides methodically that we can most definitely make our escape and help get everybody else out too."

DECISION TIME!

Do you:

A Stick with Ronald. **Go to Section24, PAGE 59**

Or

B Choose someone else. **Go to Section11, PAGE 37**

SECTION 8

Merlin The Second says:
"I used to work here for the Count as his Gardener for a while. I know a little bit about the layout of the house and I also know that the Count keeps a stash of gold coins in one of the rooms. It is worth millions and I can probably get us there. We may never have to work for a living ever again, he laughs. We can travel the world and take it easy!"

Something about his manner makes him seem a bit unreliable and not as innocent as he makes out,

DECISION TIME!

Do you:

A Stick with Merlin because the talk of treasure has you hooked. **Go to Section32, PAGE 73**

OR:

B Choose someone else. **Go to Section11, PAGE 37**

SECTION 9

Gladys says:
"I was the Nurse here at the mansion for over twelve months. I know the layout really well and I can help us escape. I have an excellently stocked first aid kit with painkillers and energy boosters just in case we need them. I know how to take good care of people - I can tell what you need just by looking at you!"

DECISION TIME!

Do you:

A Stick with Gladys because she is good at giving clear, strong direction which is what you think is required right now. You think she seems a little over-caring, though you welcome her concerns for your welfare. **Go to Section33, PAGE 74**

Or

B Choose someone else. **Go to Section11, PAGE 37**

SECTION 10

You are standing at the Drinks table. From here you can observe everyone.

You notice a slight draft around your ankles. You look behind you to see where it is coming from and you notice that one of the wooden panels in the wall is slightly ajar. You push on it to see what is behind.

It begins to open a little more though is stiff. As you push hard against the wooden panel it suddenly gives way and you stumble inside as the panel springs shut behind you and you find yourself on the other side. You immediately push back against it though it is now firmly closed tight.

Everything is black. A mist starts to develop in front of your eyes and suddenly it clears almost as quickly as it appeared to reveal a surreal landscape of trees made from candy, with sweets as fruits and grassy hills made of fondant icing. A chocolate river meanders through the scene off into the distance. You notice a candy boat at the shoreline. As you approach you see a purple elf at the helm of the boat. You ask "Can I come aboard?"

The Elf beckons you aboard with a smile.
As you take your seat and the boat takes off along the chocolate river.

You notice an onyx and brass table laden with delicious looking chocolates. You reach forward and take a few chocolates and accidentally tip the table over which immediately cracks a hole in the bottom of the boat, letting in liquid chocolate. As the crack becomes progressively worse, you shout over to the Elf to come and help you.

He is preoccupied with driving the boat and angrily taps on a sign which reads, 'Do not talk to the Elf whilst the boat is in motion'.

DECISION TIME!

Do you:

A Do your best to block the hole to stop it getting worse. **Go to Section37**, **PAGE 78**

OR:

B Challenge the Elf. Demand he fix the leak to prevent the boat from sinking. **Go to Section38, PAGE 79**

SECTION11

You find yourself back in the dining room, which may not be for the first time, but that's okay.

Maybe the typing Adventure style isn't for you, though why not give it one more try and perhaps go for slightly different preferences this time round?

The clock is ticking. Make your choice.

DECISION TIME!

Do you approach:

A The man dressed in an Armani suit with a gold Rolex watch. **Go to Section5, PAGE 30**

OR:

B The young woman with a sore foot. She has mousey unkempt hair, looking somewhat anxious. She is sitting in a chair with her shoe off, rubbing her foot. She seems to be in pain. **Go to Section6, PAGE 31**

OR:

C The geeky looking young man with instruction books. He is sitting at a table wearing a smart white shirt with a starched collar. He has a number of books around him. These are carefully arranged books. **Go to Section7, PAGE 32**

OR:

D The Rastafarian man who is middle aged, sitting back in his chair. He is wearing tie-dyed coloured clothing. He seems very relaxed and is smiling broadly. **Go to Section8, PAGE 33**

OR:

E The tall muscular Nurse who seems very fit and able. She looks about six foot tall and is wearing a starched nurse's uniform. **Go to Section9, PAGE 34**

OR:

Don't approach anyone and sit at your own table and observe. Formulate your own plan.

There are three tables to choose from. Choose your table.

F The Drinks Table

Choose The Drinks Table near the entrance which gives you a commanding view of the entire room. There is no chair but you are happy to stand. People come up occasionally to fix themselves a drink and this gives you an opportunity to engage them in conversation and find out a little about them. You can see all the comings and goings and who is talking to who. **Go to Section10, PAGE 35**

OR:

G The Reading Table

Choose The Reading Table on the left side of the room alongside the bookcase. There is a high backed wooden chair next to the table. On the wall next to this table there is a map dated 1853 that no one else has noticed. It may not be entirely up to date though gives you some knowledge of the overall layout and entrances and exits. **Go to Section14, PAGE 43**

OR:

H The Coffee Table

Choose The Coffee Table. There is a small coffee table tucked away at the back of the room with a compact armchair by the side of it. It is in a quiet corner so no one can see you though you get a general idea of what is going on in the room. **Go to Section15, PAGE 44**

SECTION 12

You lead the way through this next door. As you do so the door slams shut behind you and you find yourself on your own in a long passageway.

The door is locked and so you have no choice but to move forward along the passageway. Eventually you reach a door which you are able to open and you find yourself back in the dining room.

The door clicks shut behind you. **Go to Section11, PAGE 37**

SECTION 13

You clean the lifeboats and night falls.

You and Merlin sneak into the Captain's Cabin and successfully steal the Gold Key. As you do this, everything turns black. The mists appear and then disappear just as quickly to reveal that you and Merlin are now in a circus.

You are under the Big Top, watching the clowns clown around.

Merlin says, "Wait here a moment."

You can just about see Merlin in the dusk in the distance, talking with the Ringmaster and there seems to be an exchange going on.

Merlin returns with good news, he explains. "I have got you a job as a Clown's Assistant. It will just be one or two days at the most and then we can escape and find the treasure room and open it up with the Golden Key.

DECISION TIME!

Do you:

A Think Merlin is either some kind of Con Man or Practical Joker and you decide to take control of the situation and find your own way back to the dining room through a strange door you noticed near the entrance to the Big Top. **Go to Section12, PAGE 40**

OR:

B Give Merlin the benefit of the doubt for a day or two. **Go to PAGE 112**

SECTION 14

You notice a slight draft around your ankles. You look behind you to see where it is coming from and you notice that one of the wooden panels in the wall is slightly ajar. You push on it to see what is behind.

It begins to open a little more though is stiff. As you push hard against the wooden panel it suddenly gives way and you stumble inside as the panel springs shut behind you and you find yourself on the other side. You immediately push back against it though it is now firmly closed tight.

You find yourself in … **Go to Section42, PAGE 84**

SECTION 15

You notice a slight draft around your ankles. You look behind you to see where it is coming from and you notice that one of the wooden panels in the wall is slightly ajar. You push on it to see what is behind.

It begins to open a little more though is stiff. As you push hard against the wooden panel it suddenly gives way and you stumble inside as the panel springs shut behind you and you find yourself on the other side. You immediately push back against it though it is now firmly closed tight.

You find yourself in … **Go to Section42, PAGE 84**

SECTION 16

Gerard says I have noticed just behind us there is a door that is unlocked. If we slip out now, no one will see us. Let's go.

He opens the door and you both rush through, closing the door behind you. Everything goes black. A mist starts to develop in front of your eyes and suddenly it clears almost as quickly as it appeared.

You find yourselves in a small lifeboat next to a huge ship. The ship is sinking very slowly. There are eight sailors on board the sinking ship.

One of them shouts out, "Our radio is broken and we cannot send out an SOS signal. Can you help us?"

Somehow, in this reality, you have the knowledge to fix the radio. You know it is going to take some time to repair. Gerard tells you that you must row as fast as you can to a swirling, glowing portal which shall shortly be closing. If you stop to repair the radio the portal will close and you will fail to win the prize as this is the one opportunity you have to go through the portal.

Gerard tells you that these are experienced sailors and he is sure they will be fine without your help.

DECISION TIME!

Do you:

Give up on the prize and stay and fix the radio. **Go to Section17, PAGE 47**

OR:

Do you stay in the lifeboat with Gerard and row as hard as you can to the portal to win the prize. **Go to Section18, PAGE 48**

SECTION 17

You have made your way from the lifeboat to the Control Room on the sinking ship to fix the radio.

After an hour or so you successfully repair the radio and sent out the SOS message and help is on its way.

You make your way out of the Control Room to tell the rest of the Crew, however, as you open the door everything goes black.

A mist appears and you are transported back to **Go to Section11, PAGE 37**

SECTION 18

You both shout in delight as you make it through the portal just in time as it closes behind you.

The celebrations are short lived as there is an explosion. For a few moments, chaos is all around you as you reorient yourselves. You realise very quickly that you are on a space station which is beginning to break apart. There are a number of dead astronauts floating around.

Gerard looks at his Rolex watch and says, "We have precisely one minute fifty seconds to make it to the escape pod.

Gerard moves off quickly towards the pod. As you follow him swiftly to the pod you notice that you have lost your watch. As luck would have it, there are two watches floating right in front of you and you can easily grab one of them on your way to the pod.

DECISION TIME!

Do you:

A Take the solid gold watch that has a minimalist face though because there is no moving second hand you cannot be sure if it is operational. **Go to Section20, PAGE 51**

OR:

B Take the plastic waterproof digital watch that is definitely working as you see the seconds counting upwards. **Go to Section19, PAGE 50**

SECTION 19

You put on the plastic watch and accidentally press one of the buttons in so doing.

Everything goes black and you are transported to...
Go to Section11, PAGE 37

SECTION 20

You make it to the escape pod and put your gold watch on as Gerard fiddles with the controls. It does seem to be keeping the correct time and you feel relieved.

Gerard shouts to you to hit the red button next to your seat, quickly. As soon as you do this, the escape pod door seals behind you and the pod blasts away from the disintegrating space ship.

Everything goes black. A mist appears and then, almost immediately, disappears.

You find yourself lying on the floor in what seems to be a corridor of the Infinity Mansion. Gerard is at the end of the corridor. You notice that he opens a doorway, looks through, closes the door and then goes across to the other side of the doorway and runs up a small staircase.

He is gone for several minutes, exploring what is at the top.

When he gets back he helps you up and says, "The doorway on the left appears to lead to the street outside. At the top of the stairs is the final hurdle to the big prize, but I have to tell you, my friend, it is a dangerous route to take. It is certainly not for the faint hearted. Are you with me?"

DECISION TIME!

Do you:

A Accept the risk and push forward anyway, focusing on the determination and tenacity of your guide. **Go to PAGE 104**

Or

B Glancing at your watch, you notice it is approaching midnight. You decide to push open the escape door on the left to see if it does in fact lead to the street and to freedom, giving up on the potential prize. **Go to Section12, PAGE 40**

SECTION 21

Florence says, "There is a doorway just here, by the table. Let's go through."

The door closes behind both of you. You find yourself in a narrow passageway. You notice that she seems to be struggling with her foot so you help her along and she is limping quite badly.

Eventually you reach a small room. There is a lot of old furniture and it is all quite dusty. There is a bookcase in the corner and beside it an old fashioned wheelchair.

You suggest to Florence that she sit in the wheelchair and you push her the rest of the way. She declines and is quite stressed and adamant she wishes to continue on foot.

DECISION TIME!

Do you:

A Insist Florence sits in the wheelchair so that you can push her and she can rest her foot. **Go to Section22, PAGE 55**

OR:

B You seem to have touched a nerve and you feel that if you push it any more you may cause an argument. So you decide to leave it be and to leave the wheelchair where it is. **Go to Section12, PAGE 40**

SECTION 22

The guide eventually agrees to sit I the wheelchair and you begin pushing her through the next doorway along a long narrow passageway.

The passageway opens out into a long galley kitchen. There are double doors at the far end which you need to go and prop open so that you can push the wheelchair through.

As you are propping open the second swing door with a heavy pan, Florence shouts over to you saying, "Yum! I love lasagna!"

She is out of the chair and bending over the open door of a very large fridge.

She closes the fridge door and sits back down in the wheelchair.

DECISION TIME!

Do you:

A Push her on to the next room. **Go to Section12, PAGE 40**

OR:

B You decide to heat up one of the lasagnas for your guide. **Go to Section23, PAGE 57**

SECTION 23

You enter the next passageway and push through the next door which slams shut behind you and locks with a click.

You quickly notice that this next wide passageway is flooded and you are in ankle deep water.

You continue pushing the wheelchair harder but it is slow going and you are becoming very tired. You estimate it will take you about ten minutes to get to the end of this passageway, continuing as you are going. Your arms are already aching and you begin to notice movement in the water.

There is a shoal of hundreds of tiny fish which are now irritatingly nipping at your ankles.

DECISION TIME!

Do you:

A Push on anyway to the end of the hallway, enduring the pain. **Go to PAGE 102**

OR:

B Ask Florence to leave the wheelchair and continue on foot and both of you will be at the end of the passageway and able to step through the next door in half the time. **Go to Section12, PAGE 40**

SECTION 24

Ronald says, "According to the History Book if we find the painting on the wall in the dining room of a castle with a red flag then just below this painting there is a secret passageway.

You scan the room and in a quiet corner you see the small painting of the castle. You both approach. You reach up with your hand and feel the wooden paneling below the painting. Ronald discovers a loose piece of wood in the paneling which he presses in and a small doorway opens up in the paneling.

You both squeeze through this doorway and as you do the panel closes and locks behind you.

You are now in a small room and as you turn to get your bearings you knock a vase from a pedestal. The vase breaks into thirty or forty pieces.

Ronald says, "Oh no, the history book states that the vase in this small chamber has a code on it that will help us escape!"

DECISION TIME!

Do you:

A Patiently stick the vase back together with the glue that Ronald produces from his satchel. **Go to Section25, PAGE 61**

OR:

B You think it will be quicker and more appealing, to create a mosaic on the table, made from the pieces of the vase and whereby you can examine each piece for the code. **Go to Section26, PAGE 63**

OR:

C You think that either option will take just too much time and so you leave Ronald to put it back together by himself as you notice another door in front of you that you take to return to the dining room. **Go to Section12, PAGE 40**

SECTION 25

You have painstakingly put the vase back together to reveal the code which is 1451.

You both make your way through the door in front of you. The door slams shut and locks behind you. Everything goes black.

A mist begins to appear and then disappear almost as quickly to reveal that you are in some kind of a space ship. There are control panels either side of you.

On the screen to your left the words, 'Alpha Emergency' are flashing.

Ronald passes you the space ship Emergency Instruction Booklet.

The lights are all flashing now and there is an irritating siren which has progressed to an uncomfortable pitch.

You look up what to do in the case of an Alpha Emergency. This chapter is 52 PAGE s long.

DECISION TIME!

Do you:

A Read the chapter word for word. **Go to Section48, PAGE 93**

OR:

B Watch as Ronald slowly reads through the chapter as you stand back and observe. **Go to Section28, PAGE 67**

OR:

C Skim read the chapter for the important points. **Go to Section29, PAGE 69**

SECTION 26

You have created a beautiful mosaic to reveal the code which is 1451.

You both make your way through the door in front of you. The door slams shut and locks behind you. Everything goes black.

A mist begins to appear and then disappear almost as quickly to reveal that you are in some kind of a space ship. There are control panels either side of you.

On the screen to your left the words, 'Alpha Emergency' are flashing in fluorescent yellow lettering. Sirens are sounding at a heightened pitch which hurts your ears.

You are gripped by a tremendous fear.

Ronald passes you the space ship Emergency Instruction Booklet and tells you that you must read it carefully right now as your life depends upon it.

The lights are all flashing now and there is a second irritating siren which has progressed to an uncomfortable pitch. The situation is overwhelming in its intensity.

You cannot find the right PAGE and so Ronald comes over and opens it swiftly at the right PAGE, mumbling under his breath.

You stare at the contents PAGE and shout over to Ronald, "But this chapter on the Alpha Emergency is 52 PAGE s long!"

He shouts an angry reply, "Just read it!"

DECISION TIME!

Do you:

A Read the chapter word for word. **Go to Section48, PAGE 93**

OR:

B You forcefully hand the book back to Ronald concluding that you cannot do this. Watch as Ronald slowly reads through the chapter as you stand back and observe. **Go to Section49, PAGE 94**

OR:

C Skim read the chapter for the important points. **Go to Section29, PAGE 69**

SECTION 27

A shooting gallery in a funfair.

The funfair is not open yet so it is your job to set up the shooting gallery for opening that evening. Ronald searches around to find out why you are here.

When he gets back he tells you what he has discovered.

Ronald says, "In order for us to escape this place we need a vehicle. There happens to be a motorbike for sale. It costs $150. The Fairground Master has given me $150 to award as the Grand Target Prize here in the Shooting Gallery. If no one hits the Grand Target, we can keep the $150. We can then buy the motorbike and escape tonight under cover of darkness.

DECISION TIME!

Do you:

A Seek to sabotage the Shooting Gallery by nailing down the Grand Target, thus guaranteeing nobody wins the Grand Prize resulting in you having the $150 for the motorbike. **Go to Section29, PAGE 69**

OR:

B You feel that you will be able to come up with a more creative idea so you decide to take some time out to put your idea together while Ronald does the preparation work on the Shooting Gallery. **Go to PAGE 106**

OR:

C You run the Shooting Gallery honestly and leave it to chance. **Go to PAGE 100**

SECTION 28

You read the chapter word for word. You follow the instructions precisely and you are able to avert disaster.

However, just as you and Ronald are celebrating everything goes black.

A mist appears out of nowhere and disappears just as quickly revealing that you and Ronald are now standing in a shooting gallery in a funfair. The funfair is not open yet so it is your job to set up the shooting gallery for opening that evening. Ronald searches around to find out why you are here.

When he gets back he tells you what he has discovered.

Ronald says, "In order for us to escape this place we need a vehicle. There happens to be a motorbike for sale. It costs $150. The Fairground Master has given me $150 to award as the Grand Target Prize here in the Shooting Gallery. If no one hits the Grand Target, we can keep the $150. We can then buy the motorbike and escape tonight under cover of darkness.

DECISION TIME!

Do you:

A Seek to sabotage the Shooting Gallery by nailing down the Grand Target, thus guaranteeing nobody wins the Grand Prize resulting in you having the $150 for the motorbike. **Go to Section29, PAGE 69**

OR:

B You feel that you will be able to come up with a more creative idea so you decide to take some time out to put your idea together while Ronald does the preparation work on the Shooting Gallery. **Go to PAGE 106**

OR:

C You run the Shooting Gallery honestly and leave it to chance. **Go to PAGE 100**

SECTION 29

After taking a shortcut (some would say 'cheating') everything goes black. A mist starts to form and you are transported back to ... **Go to Section 11, PAGE 37**

SECTION 30

Everything goes black. A mist starts to develop in front of your eyes and suddenly it clears almost as quickly as it appeared.

You and Merlin find yourself on a pirate ship. Merlin says, "We must pretend to be part of the crew until nightfall, then we can sneak into the Captain's Cabin and steal the Gold Key that will give us access to the stash of golden coins.

Throughout the day orders are being shouted at you to scrub floors and polish canons. Every now and then the Captain comes out of his Cabin and inspects the work. If it is not good enough, the Captain grabs the culprit by the hair and slashes his throat in front of the entire crew. You wonder if you are going to survive until nightfall.

You are ordered to clean the lifeboats.

DECISION TIME!

Do you:

A Clean the lifeboats. **Go to Section 13, PAGE 41**

OR:

B Use this opportunity whilst nobody is looking to escape to safety in one of the lifeboats. **Go to Section31, PAGE 72**

SECTION 31

You lower the lifeboat into the water and escape whilst another one of the Crew is being tortured for not cleaning the deck adequately.

Everything goes black. A mist starts to develop in front of your eyes and suddenly it clears almost as quickly as it appeared. You are transported back to **Section11, PAGE 37**

SECTION 32

Merlin explains that there is a secret door behind the buffet that will take us into a small room. In that room there are three doors, one of which is solid gold and that is our door!

You and Merlin make your way behind the buffet and he guides you through the secret door and you both find yourselves in a small room. Sure enough, Merlin is right, there ARE three doors and one of them is gleaming gold.

You both walk up to the golden door. At this point Merlin seems to sober up and becomes deadly serious. He looks you in the eye and firmly places his hand on your back and says, "YOU go first."

DECISION TIME!

Do you:

A Enter the golden door first. **Go to Section30, PAGE 70**

OR:

B Decide to take this last chance to turn around and determinedly head back to the dining room. **Go to Section12, PAGE 40**

SECTION 33

Gladys says
"Follow me this way to the secret passageway."

You follow her behind some empty tables and chairs in a quiet corner of the dining room. She places a hand on a wooden panel and presses it and a small door opens up in the wood paneling. You both go through into the next room and the door closes behind you.

You have some doubts as to whether Gladys is a fully qualified nurse.

DECISION TIME!

Do you:

A Pretend to sprain your ankle and see how she straps it up for you to make sure she is a real nurse.
Go to Section34, PAGE 75

OR:

B You feel there is really not enough time for this and just decide to go with Gladys into the next room.
Go to Section12, PAGE 40

SECTION 34

You pretend to fall over and sprain your ankle. Gladys straps your ankle quickly and proficiently. She is obviously a true professional.

The two of you then move on into the next room.

The room is dark. You sense movement in one corner.

DECISION TIME!

Do you:

A Move to the opposite corner and freeze. **Go to Section35, PAGE 76**

OR:

B You see a sword on the wall. You grab it and start wildly brandishing it around in the direction of the movement. **Go to Section36, PAGE 77**

SECTION 35

A light comes on in the room.

In the opposite corner you can make out a person standing there. They say, "I can help you escape."

DECISION TIME!

Do you:

A Say, "I don't trust you." **Go to PAGE 110**

OR:

B Remain suspicious and wait to see how Gladys reacts before you act. **Go to PAGE 110**

OR:

C Say, "Great, let's go!" **Go to Section 12, PAGE 40**

SECTION 36

A dim light comes on in the room.

In front of your sword you can just make out a person standing right in front of you. They say, "I can help you escape."

DECISION TIME!

Do you:

A Say, "I don't trust you." **Go to PAGE 110**

OR:

B Remain suspicious and wait to see how Gladys reacts before you act. **Go to PAGE 110**
OR:

C Say, "Great, let's go!" **Go to Section12, PAGE 40**

SECTION 37

You successfully block the hole in the bottom of the boat and disaster is averted.

The boat suddenly goes into a dark cave. Everything goes black. A mist starts to form and you are transported to ... **Go to Section42, PAGE 84**

SECTION 38

The Elf eventually comes over to the leak to investigate but by then it is too late. The hole is irreparable and the boat sinks quickly.

You and the Elf swim for the shore as the boat sinks to the bottom of the chocolate river.

When you reach the shore the Elf is very angry. He is kicking the ground and shouting and blames you for the sinking of the boat.

DECISION TIME!

Do you:

A Apologise and take the blame in order to diffuse the situation. **Go to Section39, PAGE 80**

OR:

B Explain that it was NOT your fault and, if anything, it was the Elf's fault for not heeding your warning. **Go to Section40, PAGE 81**

SECTION 39

You apologise to the Elf who then calms down.

You are able to disappear into a forest of candy. You notice a small chocolate cave and you decide to explore inside.

In the cave there is ... **Go to Section42, PAGE 84**

SECTION 40

This infuriates the Elf even further and a crowd of other purple Elves appear from nowhere.

The next thing you know you find yourself under arrest and in Jail.

The Elf solicitor who has been assigned to you advises you plead 'guilty'.

If you plead guilty the worst that happens is that you have to perform one week of community service.

If you plead not guilty and you lose, you could be facing a twelve month prison sentence.

DECISION TIME!

Do you:

A Choose to plead guilty.

You are asked to offer an unreserved apology to the Elf community and accept the entire blame for the incidence.

You will be charged with reckless and foolish behavior leading to the destruction of another's property and you will be given a week's period of community service in the Land of Elves and allowed to go free thereafter. **Go to Section41, PAGE 83**

OR:

B Choose to plead not guilty.

You decide that the Elf solicitor is incompetent and you sack him and you choose to represent yourself in Elf Court. You will build a case around the fact that the Elf did not respond to your warning of potential danger fast enough and that the onyx and brass table was a hazard **Go to PAGE 114**

SECTION 41

You plead guilty and apologise to the Elves and have completed your Community Service.

You are set free and you decide to make your escape from this land down a passageway that you first saw when you arrived here. **Go to Section42, PAGE 84**

SECTION 42

A narrow passageway.

It is very dark. You manage to work your way along the winding passage until you come to a metal door, which seems to open automatically as it senses your presence, inviting you in.

You are suddenly lifted off your feet and pulled out through the door into a blackness. A mist begins to form and you are transported to ... **Go to Section43, PAGE 85**

SECTION 43

The Control Room of a space ship. There are control panels either side of you.

On the screen to your left the words, 'Low Oxygen' are flashing.

The lights are all flashing now and there is an irritating siren which has progressed to an uncomfortable pitch.

There are nine crew members scattered about the floor, drifting in and out of consciousness.

DECISION TIME!

Do you:

A Rush around putting oxygen masks on all the crew members and share your own supply with them. **Go to Section45, PAGE 89**

OR:

B Work out the controls on the control panel to try and get more information about the Emergency oxygen situation and try to get more supplied. **Go to Section44, PAGE 87**

OR:

C Head for the escape pod, to save your life, even though it will lead to separation from the rest of the crew, knowing that you tried your very best, though it turned out to be useless. **Go to Section46, PAGE 91**

SECTION 44

You are at the control panel of the space ship attempting to supply more oxygen to the control cabin. Your space suit keeps you with a good supply of oxygen at the moment, though you are struggling with the cumbersomeness of the suit in trying to operate the controls.

The lights are becoming more dim and you can no longer hear the gush of air coming through the vents. The nine crew members have almost all now become unconscious.

DECISION TIME!

Do you:

A Keep working on the control panel. **Go to PAGE 108**

OR:

B Share your oxygen supply with the crew, thereby depleting your own supply and reducing the time yours will last. **Go to Section45, PAGE 89**

OR:

C Head for the escape pod even though this will give you a sense of separation from the crew and a feeling that, even though you tried your very best, it turned out to be useless. **Go to Section46, PAGE 91**

SECTION 45

You have put oxygen masks on the crew members and shared your own with them.

A mist begins to appear and then disappear almost as quickly to reveal that you are at a friend's party.

One of the influential and overbearing guests gets quite drunk and, whilst you excuse yourself to go to the toilet, thinks it will be a great joke for everyone to ignore you when you come back into the room.

You enter the room and approach the group you have been chatting with previously who completely ignore you and continue with their own conversation.

You wander over to another person and introduce yourself and they simply walk away as you have your hand outstretched to shake theirs.

You hear a few giggles in the room and feel perplexed. You hear a comment which makes you realise what is going on. So you approach your best friend for comfort, who looks at you fleetingly and appears to be very nervous and also won't speak to you.

DECISION TIME!

Do you:

A Confront your friend and demand an explanation as to what's going on and why they are ignoring you. **Go to Section47, PAGE 92**

OR:

B Feel for your friend, being put in a difficult position and know everything will be alright tomorrow so resolve to quietly leave the party alone to avoid upset. **Go to PAGE 116**

SECTION 46

You enter the escape pod. The door seals shut behind you. The escape pod then blasts away from the doomed ship.

Suddenly everything goes black. A mist begins to form and you are transported to a small room. There is a door in front of you. **Go to Section12, PAGE 40**

SECTION 47

The next day at work you head to your colleague's office. On your way there you notice a strange door that you have never seen before. **Go to Section12, PAGE 40**

SECTION 48

You read the chapter word for word. You follow the instructions precisely and you are able to avert disaster.

However, just as you and Ronald are celebrating everything goes black.

A mist appears out of nowhere and disappears just as quickly revealing that it has transported you to ...
Go to Section27, PAGE 65

SECTION 49

As Ronald is reading the manual, you notice that a cable has become detached from an input socket on the control panel.

You hook up the cable again and the emergency is averted.

As you and Ronald are celebrating, everything suddenly goes black, a mist appears and transports you to ... **Go to Section27, PAGE 65**

Type 1
"Not following the rules is why we don't have nice things"

Kitching Whittaker Enneagram

"You can't type me. I'm a one of a kind!"
=Type 4

Kitching Whittaker Enneagram

5, the quiet Type

Kitching Whittaker Enneagram

For a good time, dial Type 7

Kitching Whittaker Enneagram

Announcing The Kitching Whittaker Character Types!

The Right One

Congratulations!

You are nearly at the end of the Adventure!

Read the following list of personality traits and note which ones you agree with about your own character.

SUMMARY:
*Conscientious and ethical with a strong sense of right and wrong.
*I am often focused on improving myself and I am wary of making mistakes.
*Orderly and fastidious.
*Highly Principled.
*Discerning and wise, realistic and noble.
*Morally Heroic.
*I have a dislike of corruption and I hate injustice.
*I have a desire to be good, to have integrity and to be balanced.
*I am sometimes known as an Idealist or good Advocate
*I feel motivated to improve everything and to be beyond criticism.

DECISION TIME!

Does this sound like you? If you have six or more of these traits, **go to the Chapter entitled 'Time to Be No.1', PAGE 257**

If not, start the adventure again and perhaps this time select other preferences you are drawn to.

The Helpful One

Congratulations!

You are nearly at the end of the Adventure!

Read the following list of personality traits and note which ones you agree with about your own character.

SUMMARY:
*Empathetic, sincere and warmhearted, sentimental
*Friendly, generous & Sometimes, self-sacrificing
*I can be very flattering
*Driven to be close to others
*Sometimes I don't acknowledge my own needs.
*Altruistic and unselfish
*I have a genuine love for others
*I don't want to feel unwanted
*I desire to feel that I am loved - it is important to me.
*People tell me I am a good host/hostess and I like to be appreciated

DECISION TIME!
Does this sound like you? If you have six or more of these traits, **go the Chapter entitled, 'Time to Help You No.2s', PAGE 259**

If not, start the adventure again and perhaps this time select other preferences you are drawn to.

The Striving for Success One

Congratulations! You are nearly at the end of the Adventure!

Read the following list of personality traits and note which ones you agree with about your own character.

SUMMARY:
*Self-assured, I am told I am attractive and charming.
*Ambitious, competent and energetic
*Status conscious and highly driven; I care about image and what others think of me
*I can be quite competitive
*I am a good role model and can inspire others.
*I like doing worthwhile things
*I am a Professional
*I appreciate nice things
*I am motivated to distinguish oneself from others, to gain attention by being the best I can be
*I do not like failing at something.

DECISION TIME!

Does this sound like you? If you have six or more of these traits, **go to the Chapter entitled 'Time to be Image Free for No.3s', PAGE 261**

If not, start the adventure again and perhaps this time select other preferences you are drawn to.

The I'm the Only One

Congratulations!

You are nearly at the end of the Adventure!

Read the following list of personality traits and note which ones you agree with about your own character.

SUMMARY:
*Self aware, sensitive and reserved
*I would call myself emotionally honest
*I can be quite self conscious
*I tend to steer away from ordinary ways of doing things and like my own space
*Sometimes I focus on my inner world quite a lot and focus on why I am so different
*I often think there is something inherently wrong with the world and worry about it
*I am creative at things I like to do though I often worry I am not good enough
*I feel motivated by true beauty
*I don't like people to intrude too much and sometimes I feel I must protect my feelings
*I vacillate between being overly involved or disinterested.

DECISION TIME!

Does this sound like you? If you have six or more of these traits, **go to the Chapter entitled 'Time to Be More For All the 4s', PAGE 263**

If not, start the adventure again and perhaps this time select other preferences you are drawn to.

The Thoughtful One

Congratulations!

You are nearly at the end of the Adventure!

Read the following list of personality traits and note which ones you agree with about your own character.

SUMMARY:
*Alert and curious, I concentrate on complexity
*Inventive but can be preoccupied
*Visionary but can be reclusive, preferring time to myself
*I like to feel I am a pioneer and innovator
*I don't like feeling I am incapable of something.
*I have a desire to be competent at whatever I am doing at the time.
*I like to solve problems.
*I am motivated to acquire knowledge and to understand my environment.
*I like to have things figured out.
*I don't like to feel under threat of something bad happening so I endeavor to be prepared.

DECISION TIME!

Does this sound like you? If you have six or more of these traits, **go to the Chapter entitled 'Time to Thrive For No.5s', PAGE 265**

If not, start the adventure again and perhaps this time select other preferences you are drawn to.

The Safe One

Congratulations!

You are nearly at the end of the Adventure!

Read the following list of personality traits and note which ones you agree with about your own character.

SUMMARY:
*Committed, security orientated
*Reliable and hardworking, responsible and trustworthy
*Quite cautious and can be indecisive
*I can be reactive and rebellious
*Hardworking Stability
*Stable and self reliant
courageously championing self and others
*I don't like feeling I don't have any support
*I like to feel secure and know what the future holds
*It is nice to have some security in life
*If I feel insecure I either get very animated and try to get a feeling of security back again or worry myself silly about it and hide away.

DECISION TIME!

Does this sound like you? If you have six or more of these traits**, go to the Chapter entitled 'Time for The Unrestrictive No.6s', PAGE 267**

If not, start the adventure again and perhaps this time select other preferences you are drawn to.

The Fun One

Congratulations!

You are nearly at the end of the Adventure!

Read the following list of personality traits and note which ones you agree with about your own character.

SUMMARY:
*Extroverted and optimistic
*Versatile and spontaneous
*Playful and high spirited
*Often very practical
*There is a danger of me becoming exhausted as I often throw myself into enthusiasm
*Focused on worthwhile goals
*I don't like being tied down
*Freedom means a lot to me
*I don't like missing out
*Keeping preoccupied to avoid serious things.

DECISION TIME!

Does this sound like you? If you have six or more of these traits, **go to the Chapter entitled 'Time to Get Out Of Heaven, No.7s', PAGE 269**

If not, start the adventure again and perhaps this time select other preferences you are drawn to.

The War One

Congratulations!

You are nearly at the end of the Adventure!

Read the following list of personality traits and note which ones you agree with about your own character.

SUMMARY:
*Self confident, strong and assertive.
*Protective and resourceful.
*Can be magnanimous, with immense compassion.
*I do not like displays of weakness, though I shall fight for and defend the less fortunate.
*Self mastering and heroic at times.
*Do not like to be harmed or controlled by others.
*I have a desire to be in charge of the unpredictable in life.
*I am motivated to display my strength when threatened.
*I like to be important and dominate the environment as I prefer to stay in charge of what happens to me as much as possible.
*Justice and honoring truth mean a lot to me.

DECISION TIME!

Does this sound like you? If you have six or more of these traits**, go to the Chapter entitled 'No Time To Infuriate the No.8s', PAGE 271**

If not, start the adventure again and perhaps this time select other preferences you are drawn to.

The Peace One

Congratulations!

You are nearly at the end of the Adventure!

Read the following list of personality traits and note which ones you agree with about your own character.

SUMMARY:
*I am generally very accepting, trusting and stable.
*Creative, optimistic and supportive of others - often putting others before myself and not good at asking for help myself.
*Sometimes too willing to go along with others to keep the peace.
*I am considered to be optimistic and I like everyone to get along - it disturbs me when they don't.
*I can be Indomitable and all embracing, bring people together and healing conflicts.
*I don't like to experience falling out with others and so do not give others cause for upset.
*People tell me I'm usually very calm - placid some say.
*I like peace and quiet though thrive on excitement too.
*It takes a great deal to make me angry, though when I reach that point I am steadfast and stoic.
*I am often the one who brings harmony and gets others to make up after arguments and fall outs.

DECISION TIME!

Does this sound like you? If you have six or more of these traits, **go to the Chapter entitled 'Time to Re-Align the No.9s', PAGE 273**

If not, start the adventure again and perhaps this time select other preferences you are drawn to.

The imprint of your soul
Kitching Whittaker Enneagram

Each one of us creates our own reality through the lens of our personality. This concept essentially means that your reality, good or bad, is your creation.

This is true for your outer reality, such as relationships and career, as well as your inner reality such as your health and your psychological wellbeing.

So, the bad news is, this is all your fault. The good news is, we can fix this!

For those of you that know the essentials of Enneagram, you will recognise some familiar topics coming up, though the Kitching Whittaker approach and its unique typing system will be refreshing new material to enhance your knowledge. Certainly, there is new, never before seen, material for you here to supplement your knowledge.

For those who are new to the Kitching Whittaker Enneagram, be prepared for a treat too, as your authors and trainers with a collective sixty years of experience, have a reputation for presenting highly complex ideas in an accessible and entertaining manner, adding their own unique style and method of interpretation to empower your life.

Going Deeper: The Beginnings of Distrust and Separation

This small chapter contains the underpinnings of the Kitching Whittaker Enneagram and whilst may be a little deep to contemplate right now, are essential to include for you.

Nevertheless, even if you skip through this detail *'Your Typing Tunnel' will prove to be one of the most useful things you ever do to understand life*, yourself and others. We are all different and this book accommodates all!

Separation

Spiritual teachings talk of all humans originating from one soul, which shattered and became separate entities. The mission is to unify the soul once again and then all pain, misery and separation will cease.

What is spoken of on higher spiritual levels is also relatable to our personalities. When we were babies we did not think of ourselves as separate Beings. As we developed and began to realise we were separate from our mother or main carer, we experienced separation anxiety when we could not see them. If they moved out of the nursery, we thought them gone forever from our reality.

During our childhood we experienced separation, or a specific 'childhood wound' on a further level. We experienced the loss of the capacity to see life as it really is, however we had to react in certain ways to cope with the world as it is and to thrive within in, protecting ourselves as best we could.

Distrust

The biggest expression of distrust is falling asleep
If we want to become awake as our spiritual friends advise, we need to become aware of all the specific reactions which are ways of expressing the state of being asleep, ie being not awake. A reaction is what each personality type uses to deal with the sense of separation.

In actual fact, to give you a sneaky preview, the ultimate vice of the dissolving 9 personality number type, is to disengage so completely to their own needs, to confrontation and to conflict that they simply switch off, detach and, well, sleep.

Each number does their coping in a very particular way and has ways of dealing with frustration, conflict and getting out of their traps.

You hear about the process to awakening to spirituality or to the 'real self' and it can be a practical step by step process with the help of this book.

We can recognise our reaction to separation and distrust, learning to disengage those reactions in order to know the truth, rather than disengaging our essential and real self.

Here is a list of how each Enneagram type has specifically reacted since separation. Whilst you may still not yet be certain of your type (and the following chapters will serve to give you confirmation) please note that we all have reacted against this separation in specific ways, ie with one of the following reactions.

Reactions to Separation

1 has localised **rightness** (there is something wrong with you and the world);

2 has separated **Will** (they are feeling humiliated);

3 has separated **doing** (they are feeling helpless);

4 has separated **identity** (they feel abandoned and disconnected);

5 has separated **self** (they feel painful isolation);

6 has **no true nature** of self (they feel fearful insecurity);

7 has separated the **unfolding** of life (they feel lost and not knowing what to do);

8 has created **duality** (they experience guilt and badness);

9 has localised **love** (unified love went away and they have a sense that they are unloveable).

Having reacted to separation in a specific way, it becomes the lens we look through throughout life. Then, we experience a specific delusion as a result.

Delusions

So, in separation, we split further and became deluded!

1 thinks that reality is split between good and bad
2 thinks I have a separate personal Will
3 thinks I am a separate doer to all else
4 thinks I have a separate identity
5 thinks I am a separate self entirely
6 thinks I have no true nature
7 thinks I have a separate personal unfoldment
8 thinks reality is conflictual
9 thinks that love is local and split

Each of the above is an expression of the loss of unity and goodness. Have you heard the term that love unites? Love conquers all? Fix the love and you begin to bring it all together.

This forms the basis for all the chapters that follow, which will give you more clues and confirmations about your type. When you have your character type confirmed, *you will then have the tools to free yourself* from the sense of separation and delusion and progress to the way forward section at the back of this book.

Important Folks and Written Records

Here we go then with a bit of information about the important folks of the Enneagram.

All the way back in AD 375 a Greek Philosopher called **Evagrius** proposed 'the 8 evil thoughts' which it is generally accepted was the seed of the Enneagram. Also it was used by Pope Gregory the Great as the basis of his seven deadly sins.

George Gurdieff (1870) founded a school of thought known as the Fourth Way. Gurdieff was an Armenian mystic having learnt from a secret Middle Eastern School immersed in teachings from two thousand years' hence. There was no personality typing at this point.

Teaching centred around the idea that there are three brains which dominate human behaviour. These three brains are centred in the Gut, the Heart and the Intellect. These form the three Triads of the Enneagram.

This is where we begin. You will see that the 'Triads' form the first part of your Typing Tunnel.

Do you think of yourself as an instinctual person, often acting out of instinct and then maybe regretting it later? We all operate from all three aspects of the Triads, though one is usually paramount. I warn you now, that it is notoriously difficult to type yourself and it is usually by reflection and pondering on the ideas and opinions others have to you that the typing begins. However, it is so very easy to type other people!

Yes! I advise that you resist the temptation to categorise yourself too quickly (particularly from some sort of quickie internet quiz) for two important an crucial reasons: 1) because you may get it wrong or 2) you may give up in your jubilation that you've figured it all out and so will stop striving to learn more. This Kitching Whittaker typing system is so very much more than that. Please continue.

Oscar Ichazo applied the Enneagram to a system of personality typing in 1968.

In 1970 a group from the Eselen Institute spent nine months with Ichazo and began disseminating his Enneagram ideas worldwide.

Claudio Naranjo was a student of Ichazo's teachings. Medically trained in psychiatry he became the first official teacher of the Enneagram in the United States in 1971.

Naranjo promoted the idea that the figure of the Enneagram maps reality in its various manifestations and dimensions which originated in the ancient school, akin to Kabbalah.

Enneagram can be perceived as pertaining to the ego experience relating to Fixations and Passions and can be perceived on another level as reflecting spiritual enlightenment relating to the Virtues and the Holy Ideas. Thus the map becomes multidimensional and more of a mandala than a flat diagram.

Don Riso, Helen Palmer and Robert Ochs were students of Naranjo. Ochs was a Jesuit Priest and taught other Jesuits resulting in the Vatican issuing a warning in 2003. Each began publishing their works in the 1980s.

Jennie Kitching and Brit KS Whittaker then took the Enneagram to another level in 2017 by incorporating their many years of experience as counselors and hypnotherapists with a wide variety of clients. Their emphasis is on the secret programs that run our lives which can either self-sabotage or empower us.

The Devil Made Me Do It!

Enneagram and the Kabbalah

Anyone who has learned anything about the workings of the mind, particularly counseling, mentalism or hypnotherapy, recognises that often the patterns in our lives seem to escape reason.

Our dilemma often is 'tell me... why on earth do I continue to do this thing that I consciously do not want to do anymore?!'

We open up the whole debate of 'determinism' and 'chaotic free will' : do you choose to believe that your life is predetermined and written in the stars for you to act out or do you believe that your life is created moment by moment by each decision, action and thought you conjure?

Can we solve this argument by suspending our judgements and considering that both approaches could possibly be true?

The Tree of Life from the mystical tradition of the Kabbalah and this Enneagram from further back into Greek philosophy we can dare to tread, offer some insights and explanations.

From here we speak in terms of energies, not behaviour.

It saddens me that folks so quickly rush to the internet and 'type' themselves, satisfied, or dissatisfied with their findings and then discard the rest of the information in smugness or defiance!

You see, the same energy can be interpreted in different ways and this is where we are truly magical, individual Beings.

For example, a typical type 9 person sitting quietly at the dinner party may be interpreted as shy by one personality type and rude by another. Trust me. I'm a 9!

'Ah, someone go talk to Jennie, she's all on her own', or 'Well, if she doesn't want to be bothered joining in, then leave her be, you think she'd make the effort, how rude!'

The 9 might be just contemplating the deliciousness of the dessert, or silently pleading the 8 to shut up and leave them alone, who knows!

A 7 might find adventure and pleasure saturation in a bowl of custard, a forbidden drug, or challenging themselves to conquer the peak of the next mountain, who knows!

Whilst the Kabbalah depicts and explains energies and their polarities at a micro and macro level, the Enneagram focusses on how those energies are expressed from a personality viewpoint. The destructive energy of Geburah, for example, can work its way into expression in the 9 as a shutting down, a retreating, whilst the 8 can utilise it to feel more alive and thrive upon stripping down old outworn systems and implementing the new dynamism of change.

Ultimately, the Kabbalah teaches at its fundamental level that only two things exist. 1) the Creator and 2) the Creature.

The Creature (us) is focused upon receiving pleasure and does so in a variety of ways. It also seeks to avoid pain – at all costs. The fall from Grace happened when the Creature sought to be like the Creator.

In striving so hard to be Creator-like the Creature forgot/denied the Creator existed and thus began an emptiness, a profound loneliness – a separation from all else.

In our attempts to heal the wound of this separation, which began with the biggest wound of all, in childhood, we developed our personalities.

Of course, you can spot differing personalities in little children quite early on, though the negative part of the personality, the contriving, the manipulating, the power playing parts of us, grew over time, so that we could co-exist in an envious and competitive world.

We fell.   We fell into one of 9 categories, or types of personality.

Your Evolving, Revolving, Dissolving Self

You may know yourself pretty well by now and there may be some aspects of your personality that you admit and adore and live your life by.

Life is lived in comparison with our fellow Beings and the quickest way to knowing yourself well is by how you judge how others seem to be behaving. When you describe yourself as 'I'm the kind of person who....' or 'I would NEVER do a thing like that!' then you are recognising the qualities of your essential self – OR the idealistic version of yourself.

Your Evolving Self

Now, when life is hunky dory and you are feeling on top of the world, chances are you are in a state of Evolving. Some say this is the true meaning of life; to keep moving forward, despite setbacks, to forge ahead even when the world seems against you. Evolving can be very pleasant, or it can be hell on earth though evolving is the true aim of the Universe, of which you are part.

You will have your number type, though also the number that you evolve to - evolving to the very BEST of that number.

Your Revolving Self

This is where you live most of the time, often going around and around in circles, thinking thoughts you thought yesterday and getting the same reactions you would expect from your relationship to money, the environment, your own body and other people – unless you are far more enlightened than most and committed to improving yourself and your condition the majority of the time.

Your Dissolving Self

When the stresses and strains of life become too much to bear, we retreat into negative states. Those negative states are familiar and well worn and if particular patterns keep repeating in your life then you know this cycle all too well.

Happily, the Enneagram provides you with a map. This enables you to recognise your numbered personality 'type' and typically those behaviours thoughts and feelings you retreat to when anxious, upset, angry or apathetic, for example.

You will have the number given that you dissolve to - dissolving to the very WORST of that number.

Unwanted Behaviour

We can no more easily halt our unwanted behaviour patterns any more than we can prevent our hand being pulled spontaneously from something hot, or tickly, or sharp. Berating an unwanted behaviour is one small step away from berating ourselves.

We are not our Behaviours

In the same way as we would instinctively pull that hand away from the hot flame or sharp pin, so we instinctively react to circumstance when under undue stress.

Everyone is the same? Know Thyself

We may all share certain characteristics, though we all have our differing personalities and as we grow older and begin to accept our talents and flaws, these traits become more apparent.

It's Just Me!

This is what your Negative Ego (which does not want you to know that everything is indeed ONE and that hating your brother is hating yourself, ultimately) would have you believe.

It wants you to think that you are special, you are alone, you are the only one and no one has or is suffering or has had it as hard as you have.

You are a Number!

Nooooooo! 'I am not a number, I am a free man', comes the cry. There was a time, like most of my life, when I would have argued against this. I hated being categorised and yet it is so helpful when you do place yourself on this map. When you recognise the energies at work upon you and how to rise above them, or chose to accept them and wallow in the understanding(!) is a huge relief.

Enlightenment

It's like a light goes on; the penny drops. I found it easier to place myself on the map when I admitted my dissolving state; how I behave when overwhelmed with stress.

Then I had lots of reflections back at me when mentioning my findings to others, who, by the way, can serve as a mirror of ourselves.

Comments such as, 'Oh yes! You do that ALL the time and it drives me crazy', gives you the realisation that perhaps you are on the right lines.

'Absolutely not! You might like to think that, BUT what you really do when something doesn't go your way is....', means you may have to revisit the map!

Finding Direction

This Kitching Whittaker Enneagram is far more than mere 'personality typing' as it gives you a clear direction in how to progress your personality into a positive direction, using your drives and instincts and propelling yourself into that evolving desired state.

At the very least you can go lick your wounds in the corner and realise that you know yourself far better than you used to and that if the map can be right about this awful stuff you feel right now, then perhaps it is worth some time and interest to explore.

What a Coincidence! We happen to be on the very same planet at the very same time!

Of course you are not alone. Even if you wanted to be, sooner or later you have to interact with others, when you can then judge them for being nice and helpful or bloody minded and obstructive. This again, will point you to your number type and be helpful in empathising with others and/or dissociating more from them if you wish!

Mood Swings

As we are all various personality types, 9 in total, being affected by circumstance and fluctuating energies constantly, it is a wonder that any of us get along with each other at all! Yet we do. In fact, there are certain individuals we spend a whole lifetime with, often understanding and making allowances for their varying moods and tantrums far more than we will ever tolerate of ourselves.

Your Typing Tunnel

Verifying Your Number Type

Here is more information to verify your character type. Do this next section of the book to see how your typical behaviours and attitudes, beliefs and values impact on the choice you have made and further confirm your choice of type. Or, let's see how maybe you wish to try another number on for size until you find your true fit. The important thing here is that YOUR decision will equal YOUR numbered personality type.

IMPORTANT: There are *Ten Sections* within the Tunnel. At the end of each section make a note of your preferred choice, as there is an answer PAGE in the Chapter 'YOUR DECISION = YOUR NUMBER!' **PAGE 2**35, which will reveal your number type based on your preferences. Have fun!

1.Find Your Triad

The Enneagram is split into three distant triads and each one has its own unique qualities.

Now, we are all invested in all three triads, in that we all have a bit of genuine gut instinct from time to time and we all have a heart and can be very feeling and of course, we all use our head! However, there is one that is MORE influential than the others.

I shall describe them below and then you must choose the one triad you are most drawn to.

The Gut

If I am in this triad I shoot first and ask questions later!

I can have flashes of intense energy and often experience 'knee jerk' reactions to life.

People have sometimes said to me 'Why don't you just THINK before you do things?' Or, 'SEE! I told you to be more careful!' Or, 'Can't you just sit down for a moment!' Or, 'I thought you were all enthusiastic yesterday - and now you really don't seem bothered at all, what happened?'

The body is really important me, which is either utilised greatly with lots of emphasis on how things taste and smell and the pleasure the body can give, or conversely (because of the sensations of the body that this triad is more sensitive to than other triad types) they seek to anaesthetise themselves by using food or alcohol to deaden oneself to that sensitivity, or to cope with having to 'ignore' the body's messages if having to work long hours for example.

I usually take practical action, even if others disagree, because I think I am doing the right thing, or that I HAVE to do SOMETHING here even if it is NOT the right thing, or distract myself from what is going on. I sometimes just go off and DO things and maybe try to surprise other people spontaneously and I think they will be delighted and sometimes they are more shocked than pleased! I can change my mind in an instant and sometimes regret it.

I want to have impact on the world and experience true rage, if I allow myself to accept that, which is often modified into resentment or an enforced 'it doesn't really matter' attitude to save me from fully admitting just how annoying something is!

As I focus on the world and folks around me, I can be somewhat 'self forgetting'.

DECISION TIME!
Does this sound like you? If yes, make a note of 'The Gut', if not, disregard and move to next section.

The Head

If I am in this triad I am very aware of what could possibly happen that I think and plan to safeguard against bad things happening and plot my way to more pleasurable status.

I am quite a relational person and am full of ideas.

I think THEN act and I figure things out. The mental realm is important to me, finding our information (whether to find more pleasure or safeguard against danger or to further my knowledge bank). I need to have enough, or more than enough. There is fear, pain and doubt in the world and thinking it through can somewhat compensate for that.

People sometimes say to me, 'So have you decided what you are going to do yet?' Or, 'Surely to goodness you know that by now, let's go!' Or, 'We will figure it out when we get there'. Or, 'Oh, right, another one of your bright ideas, eh?'

DECISION TIME!

Does this sound like you? If yes, make a note 'The Head', if not, disregard and move to next section.

The Heart

If I am in this triad I am quite aware of how I am feeling most of the time and take steps to address those feelings.

I am alert to how others feel about me too and want to be acknowledged and thought of as significant in life.

I don't like being made a fool of and insults and criticisms hit me hard. I experience shame quite easily so I guard against it by being someone that other people like, respect and admire.

It is quite easy for me to be what is required at the time, the focused and diligent worker, the avid helper or by being very different to the norm, being the best at my endeavor. This is important to me.

In big decisions, I need to feel it is the right thing for me, though my head tells me one thing, if it doesn't FEEL right then it really bothers me.

DECISION TIME!

Does this sound like you? If yes, make a note 'The Heart'.

DECISION TIME: WHICH TRIAD ARE YOU?

GUT

HEAD

HEART?

NOTE DOWN YOUR ANSWER. You will need your answer for determining your type at the end of the Tunnel where all the answers are given.

Want to skip ahead for a sneaky peak to see the answers? ***Go to the Chapter entitled 'YOUR DECISION = YOUR NUMBER!' PAGE 235***

2. Getting Stuck on Fixations

Each number type has a particular fixation.

This section will help you find yours, which will be incredibly useful to you, so that you can recognise when you are fixating and then move along from it.

A fixation is a preoccupying idea, it is where we continually get stuck. We may be going along okay, then pow! Here we go again into our problem. It is as if each number has its own particular poisons and prisons and if we go there, we get stuck.

The reason why we get stuck is that we cannot chart our escape because it seems so very real to us. When we know what our own personal poisons and prisons are, we have an advantage. Yes, we shall argue a little, or a lot, first we others of course, then with ourselves.

Sooner or later it will just seem too much of a coincidence that every time THIS happens life begins to be frustrating, insurmountable, overwhelming. THEN some good natured soul comes along and wonders why you are all in a lather about something so unimportant when there are so many other things to worry about...!

So here is a list of poisons and prisons, have a look which may relate to your own outlook.

Fixate On Your Poisons and Prisons

We all feel the various elements of this following list, ie we all experience 'resentment' from time to time. The way to find your personal poison is to realise that when you go there, you end up in prison! That is, you get trapped - you feel negative, your power goes, you end up in a bad, bad mood and folks don't want to be around you and you most probably don't want to be around other folks.

So, as you will have experience of ALL of these, pick the ONE that you know is the biggie for you - the one that means the most, that you perhaps **fixate** upon.

DECISION TIME!
Time to note down which relates to you most.

Resentment: feeling an obligation to do the right thing while others seem to be apathetic, amoral or immoral.

Flattery: feeling an urge to pay compliments or special attention to others so that they like us or see us in a favourable light.

Vanity: feeling that one's appearance, qualities, abilities, achievements, etc. are crucial to one's place in the world and needing feedback to validate.

Melancholy: feeling a strong sense of lacking emotional fulfilment and despairing of what is missing.

Hoarding: feeling a need to hold onto resources and to minimise one's own needs in an attempt to compensate for a world that seems to take more than it gives.

Cowardice: feeling a tendency to either **succumb** to or to **challenge fears** or doubts that arise from uncertainty.

Planning: feeling that one's focus ought to be future based, looking to what COULD happen and improve and living in future anticipation of more enjoyable alternatives to present situations.

Vengeance: feeling that the world is taking advantage of the vulnerable and it is up to you to stand strong and assertive for them AND for you.

Indolence: feeling that the needs of the others outweigh YOUR OWN needs.

Now, I KNOW it is tempting to just keep reading on and see if this book becomes more interesting, though I promise you the interest will come faster and more powerfully if you sto for a moment and REALLY ponder on these fixations before moving into your trap!

DECISION TIME: WHAT IS YOUR FIXATION?

RESENTMENT

FLATTERY

VANITY

MELANCHOLY

HOARDING

COWARDICE

PLANNING

VENGEANCE

INDOLENCE

NOTE DOWN YOUR ANSWER. You will need your answer for determining your type at the end of the Tunnel where all the answers are given.

Want to skip ahead for a sneaky peak to see the answers? ***Go to the Chapter entitled 'YOUR DECISION = YOUR NUMBER!' PAGE 235***

3.Find Your Trap

Lack and Disconnection with Source

Everyone develops a method of compensating for the lack, the emptiness within the centre of the ego.

This is likened to the 'fall from grace' – that the very fact that we chose to incarnate into flesh and bone means we disconnect from Source/God/Goddess/All that Is in order to experience life anew and evolve.

The Holy Ideas

Each personality type, each one of the nine personality types, have a Fixation and a Passion (sin).

The Passions are the emotional underpinnings of each type and arise out of a background of loss of connection and a seeking to reconnect in a human way. For example, the 9 seeks reconnection to Love and Peace so aims to create it on the outer, sensing the lack on the inner.

Still with me? What this means is that all that stuff, whether from a quantum perspective or in a spiritual context, you have read about your experience really being a reflection of what is going on inside you is explained right here.

A number type '1' for example, sensed early on in life that there was something really really wrong with the world. They are right, aren't they? We all feel it. Though the 1s fixate upon it. As children, coming from a place of perfection, we discovered suddenly to our horror that the world is not perfect and sought in our way to remedy it.

The 1s sought to do this by 'doing the right thing'. Trouble is, the right thing can be different according to the number doing the perceiving, so the 1s have the burden of trying to put the world to rights by being right, doing right and having others do the right thing too, with the dilemma inside themselves that they are not perfect and continually striving to be so.

The traps lead back to your particular fixation.

Here is a list of the traps; see which one most resonates with you. At the end of the section, choose one and make a note of that choice.

DECISION TIME!

Time to find out which resonates most with you and make a note.

I am a Perfectionist

perfection strives to meet perceived standards of right and wrong in order to be acceptable.

I love Freedom

freedom from personal needs allows one to focus on the needs of others in order to feel needed and liked.

I am Efficient

efficiency produces results and achieves goals that prove one's worth.

I am Authentic

authenticity is derived from being true to an inner emotional reality that distinguishes oneself from others.

I am a keen Observer

observing the world by pulling back from it in order to gain a more objective understanding of it.

I like my Security

security seeks certainty in a future full of negative possibilities requiring a cautious or reactive response to perceived threats.

I am an Idealist

idealism reframes reality by paying attention to what's positive or interesting while avoiding what's negative or problematic.

I want Justice

justice exposes hidden truths and redresses the balance by confronting and asserting oneself against others.

I am a Seeker

seeking to understand from the viewpoint of others to merge and become one in order to be part of something greater than oneself.

DECISION TIME: WHAT IS YOUR TRAP?

PERFECTION

FREEDOM

EFFICIENCY

AUTHENTICITY

OBSERVATION

SECURITY

IDEALISM

JUSTICE

SEEKING

NOTE: The Antidote to your particular trap, which appears later in this book, address your particular trap and so help you to chart your escape.

NOTE DOWN YOUR ANSWER. You will need your answer for determining your type at the end of the Tunnel where all the answers are given.

Want to skip ahead for a sneaky peak to see the answers? ***Go to the Chapter entitled 'YOUR DECISION = YOUR NUMBER!' PAGE 235.***

4.Find Your Sin

There's nothing good here!

Bless yourself, for you have sinned - and the antidotes will be given to you towards the end of this book, honest!

When you acknowledge your particular sin/passion, you can really move on up a level and sort some things out in life and be happier.

Choose one. Yes, we may be guilty of several, or maybe you think you are not guilty of any(!), though, come on, choose one, okay?

The sins/passions were described as the result of a lack in the corresponding virtue.

With the Enneagram personality types they can be thought of as pointing to an underlying habit of emotional energy.

They've also been called the 7 sins + 2. This refers to the seven deadly, capital, or cardinal sins (anger, pride, envy, avarice, gluttony, lust, and laziness).

With the passions, the sin of lust was changed to excess and the two passions of deceit and fear were added to make nine. Below is one interpretation of how these passions apply to each Enneagram personality type.

DECISION TIME!

Time to find out which is your biggest sin.

Anger

Anger is an energy that arises in service of correcting things that don't match an internalised sense of rightness. It can be noticed in the form of criticism of things not being done correctly.

Pride

Pride is a self-inflated feeling of importance in the lives of others, coming from a feeling of being needed or indispensable in some way.

Often it arises out of the belief that I have no needs but am able to satisfy the needs of others.

Deceit

Deceit is a packaging of oneself in order to successfully sell oneself to others. The authentic self aside from the packaging is often lost in the image produced by the presentation.

Envy

Envy notices how others have what I don't because others are more than I am or have more than I do. It's a comparison of the positive in others with the negative in the self. It can expand to envy of our own past self, longing for what is lost.

Avarice

Avarice is a greed not for wealth but for time and space to process the world through the intellect.

It's a response to a world that can seem at times intrusive, chaotic, and overwhelming.

Fear

Fear is often a generalised mistrust of what and how others are thinking. This may be allayed by a questioning in search of certainty or an action that confronts the perceived fear.

Gluttony

Gluttony of the mind is a desire to taste life in all its offerings. The mind imagines an endless stream of appealing possibilities with the challenge of how to experience them all with limited time.

Excess

Excess is one of pursuing intensity or honesty of experience that feels more real and energising. For others this intensity is often felt as too much, requiring the need to sit on the energy so as not to overwhelm others.

Laziness

Laziness is an inertia seeking and maintaining comfort, averse to conflict and disruption. It's losing oneself in routines or activities that allow one to just be without having any goals to strive for or expectations to meet.

DECISION TIME: WHAT IS YOUR SIN?

ANGER

PRIDE

DECEIT

ENVY

AVARICE

FEAR

GLUTTONY

EXCESS

LAZINESS

NOTE DOWN YOUR ANSWER. You will need your answer for determining your type at the end of the Tunnel where all the answers are given.

Want to skip ahead for a sneaky peak to see the answers? ***Go to the Chapter entitled 'YOUR DECISION = YOUR NUMBER!' PAGE 235.***

5.Find Your Wound

This is of great importance. I know everyone has a wound and not many of us like to talk about it, though the people who state they have had a wonderful upbringing are few and far between.

This is very interesting, because no matter how diligent and attentive a person was as a parent or carer, the child will remember when they were having an 'off day'!

So, yes, the childhood wound is a perception. I do not wish to make light of it because it has shaped our very identity, though it is important here that this is how we perceived life as a child and that siblings of the same family can view the very same events totally differently ie this may not have been how your parents or significant carers (teachers, social workers, authority figures etc) actually treated you, more likely it is how we thought we were treated from our inexperienced and vulnerable perspective.

DECISION TIME!
It is time to contemplate your childhood and note which of the following resonates most with you, so that you can help yourself progress.

There are nine wounds.

Wound of Being Evil or Corrupt

At some critical point in my development I was heavily criticised, punished and told/felt just not good enough. I wasn't sure of the rules, or those rules got changed and I couldn't keep up. I couldn't do right for doing wrong.

I became focussed upon being good and not making mistakes to avoid my actions and behaviours being condemned by others. The message I heard was 'must do better, must do better'.

This resulted in my focus of attention to be dominantly externalised on what is wrong or imperfect about life and certain situations and what is wrong in others. I became an expert in spotting what can be made better and I became compliant to the rules of what is right and what is wrong - and what can be fixed and how it can be fixed. I inherently know how to make something better and sometimes cannot understand how this is not obvious to others. I also became focused on my own competency and being the best I could be at doing things right.

DECISION TIME!

Does this sound like you? If yes, make a note of 'Evil or Corrupt', if not, disregard and move to next one.

Wound of Being Unloved or Unwanted

When I helped someone close to me I was so enamoured by their gratitude that I really felt their love wash all over me and it felt wonderful.

I was told I was a 'good girl' or 'good boy' and I revelled in this. My own needs felt a bit selfish as I tuned them out to focus on the feelings and needs of other people. I found that even though I continued to help or try to please others, I never really felt it returned in that same way and so I keep trying. The message I heard was, 'if you are loving you will be loved'.

This resulted in my focus of attention to be externalised on others and me becoming somewhat compliant, generally speaking, as it is easy for me to be what the other person needs at the time. So, if someone needs me to do something for them, even though I was planning to do something particularly for myself, I often find myself putting them first.

I also became focused on maintaining a positive outlook, often cheering other people up. I see myself as quite 'selfless' and I act for the greater good of all.

DECISION TIME!
Does this sound like you? If yes, make a note of 'Unloved or Unwanted', if not, disregard and move to next section.

Wound of Being Worthless or Without Value

At a critical time in my development I felt suddenly loved, recognized and rewarded for some achievement I had made. I was told how well I had done and it felt wonderful. My feelings were not valued, I thought, though my performance and how well I actually DID something and what I accomplished was revered and honoured and what was expected of me mattered to me.

This disrupted me being loved for just being me rather than what I achieved and I grew to want admiration rather than love.

This resulted in my focus of attention going to me doing the most productive things and getting quickly to the goal, being the best, winning the prize. I constantly measure myself against a standard I have set and I evaluate how well I am doing, regardless of when others tell me to let up a little. The image others have of me is important.

I am not slow in coming forward and am known to be quite assertive in seeking what I want in life. The message I heard was 'if you snooze, you lose'.

I am efficient and very productive, sometimes to my detriment, in terms of energy and health and personal relationships. Being worthy matters to me.

DECISION TIME!

Does this sound like you? If yes, make a note of 'Worthless or Without', if not, disregard and move to next section.

Wound of Being Special

At a critical time in my childhood I felt suddenly abandoned by one or both parents/carers.

I was all alone and completely cut off from everyone for no fault of my own. I did not understand why. I was not seen or acknowledged and realised how very different I was from my parents/carers.

As I was so alone, I turned inwards and used my imagination for company and examined my own feelings and found a way to cope.

This disrupted me being present in the here and now as I focused on what was and what could be. I just know there is something missing - something important and that has become my focus.

I often go into what others may call a fantasy realm, though it is real to me. The inner landscape of my feelings is especially important and seeks expression.

I tend to overreact as a response to being left, or abandoned and I seem to seek it out and even cause it to happen as I expect it to.

I am sometimes withdrawn, because I choose to be, as the outer world doesn't live up to my expectations. Being different matters to me. I hate to think I might be just like everyone else.

DECISION TIME!

Does this sound like you? If yes, make a note of 'Being Special', if not, disregard and move to next section.

Wound of Being Incapable or Incompetent

When I was young I felt like I didn't receive the warmth and affection I needed from my parents or carers.

Either that, or I rejected the over-controlling parents I had who bombarded me with intrusive attention I just couldn't get away from. Either way, the affection and attention was an issue.

I felt exposed and absolutely defenseless so I constructed my defenses of mental structures to go into my own head and focus of my examination of details of the world.

This gets reflected out into the world as attention to detail, searching for some knowledge, some expertise that is not within myself so it must be out there somewhere and it will keep me safe.

The message I heard was 'keep yourself to yourself and others won't be able to intrude and attack'.

This resulted in me having an internal focus of attention as I get worried about what others want from me. I disconnect from my feelings and try to figure it all out mentally and maybe I can find a way of avoiding intensity and hurt.

In the mental realm of my mind I have found a oasis of calm which gives me feelings of security if I can only find out what I need to know.

I focus also on being totally competent at things because deep down I suspect I am inadequate and people will find that out.

DECISION TIME!

Does this sound like you? If yes, make a note of 'Incapable or Incompetent', if not, disregard and move to next one.

Wound of Being Without Support or Guidance

I was raised in an unpredictable situation and never really felt safe.

I didn't feel protected and really had no one to turn to. I began to doubt that I ever WOULD be safe and couldn't rely on it even when it was there for me. I couldn't trust my own inner guidance and instincts because they had been wrong to trust my parents or carers who were not reliable or there for me when I needed to feel protected from the dangers of the world.

I am often looking for what is safe and what is NOT safe. Sometimes I have really trusted in something only to find, yet again, it lets me down.

I am vigilant, always on the lookout for what might go wrong and I connect with others who think likewise and together we put the world to rights.

I do not trust people easily and when I do and they let me down that really affects me deeply. I find others often have a hidden agenda and I am on the lookout for it. I am a really good investigator and often test folks out in their loyalty to me, hardly believing they are what they say they are. Though when I trust you, you are my friend for life.

This has made me a very compliant person and I ingratiate myself easily with others and groups that I want to be part of. I have worries that I cannot stand alone - that it is a scary world out there.

The message I heard was 'there is safety in numbers'.

I am quick to respond when I think I am attacked, either by rushing in headlong to stop it getting worse, or by defending against any advances on my safety.

DECISION TIME!

Does this sound like you? If yes, make a note of 'Without Support or Guidance', if not, disregard and move to next one.

Wound of Being Trapped or In Pain

As a child I didn't think I was nurtured or that it wasn't enough - it didn't last for long or wasn't intense enough. As I was deeply hurt by this lack of intimacy and nurture, love and support, I sought to distract myself from it rather than wallow in self pity.

I learnt to nurture myself, by finding things to involve my senses and satisfy my desires to numb any pain and fear I was feeling. I distracted myself and learnt how to feel good and stay positive and learnt not to need it from anyone or anything else other than what I could conjure myself.

The message I heard was 'there is always more and more is better'.

This caused me to focus on external things rather than what is going on inside of me, jumping from one fun distracting thing to another, imagining more and more pleasant and pleasurable things to experience. I am assertive and why not? Why hold back when there is so many pleasurable things to experience in the world? People love me because I am always full of energy when I want to be around them and always focusing on the positive, because there is always something better around the corner.

DECISION TIME!

Does this sound like you? If yes, make a note of 'Trapped or in Pain', if not, disregard and move to next one.

Wound of Being Hurt or Controlled

These children did not receive the traditional nurturing that was needed at a vulnerable time in their development - though they were looked after and cared for perhaps, the nurturing element was lacking. The environment was emotionally and maybe even physically challenging. Any requirement for that nurturing was treated as a weakness and they were probably told to 'buck their ideas up' or advised to get over it, far too soon for their age.

They may have felt vulnerable in a controlled setting where that weakness was used against them as they were taught to be tough or suffer the consequences.

This caused their attention to be external, to search reality for where is the power, who has it and how do I get it. Who is friendly and who is my enemy, I must find out and find out quickly with high levels of energy and domination, else they find out my weakness.

I was hurt by the absence of the maternal influence and I take that hurt out into the world as I didn't know what to do with it.

I am assertive, of course I am, why wouldn't I be, hear me roar! I shall display my strength to you so you don't even think of attacking me.

Anything I perceive as a potential threat of any kind, shall be a reason to assert my dominance and let the battle commence.

The message I heard was, 'kill or be killed'.

DECISION TIME!
Does this sound like you? If yes, make a note of 'Hurt or Controlled', if not, disregard and move to next one.

Wound of Separation and Loss

These are the children who felt neglected, overlooked, ignored and they dealt with it well, by blending into the background and not drawing attention to themselves as they felt unimportant and lost.

They were attacked for having needs and expressing themselves and their anger was deemed selfish and unnecessary so they resolved to keep hidden and focus on everyone else instead.

As a result, their focus became almost externalised as they sought to improve everyone else's condition. They then didn't get into trouble for addressing their own development and desires.

They found a unique way of dissolving into the background right in front of your very eyes as others could continue conversations without seeming to notice their lack of contribution or true opinion. They find a way to dissociate from you in the middle of an interaction in order to keep themselves from imploding.

You often find them instructing you not to worry about them or that it really doesn't matter when, ultimately, it does.

They are one of the most positive characters you could ever wish to meet, always philosophical and reassuring you that things will always get better.

DECISION TIME!
Does this sound like you? If yes, make a note of 'Separation or Loss', if not, disregard and move to next one.

DECISION TIME: WHAT IS YOUR WOUND?

THINKING I'M EVIL OR CORRUPT

THINKING I'M UNWANTED OR UNLOVED

THINKING I'M WORTHLESS OR WITHOUT VALUE

THINKING I'M NOT SPECIAL

THINKING I'M INCAPABLE OR INCOMPETENT

THINKING I'M UNSUPPORTED OR WITHOUT GUIDANCE

THINKING I'M TRAPPED OR IN PAIN

THINKING I'M HURT OR CONTROLLED

THINKING I'M SEPARATED OR FEELING LOSS

NOTE DOWN YOUR ANSWER. You will need your answer for determining your type at the end of the Tunnel where all the answers are given.

Want to skip ahead for a sneaky peak to see the answers? ***Go to the Chapter entitled 'YOUR DECISION = YOUR NUMBER!' PAGE 235.***

6.Harmonic Patterns : How We Handle Our Frustrations

When frustrated, human beings react in one of three ways.

The way in which you usually react is partly how you determine what number you are.

DECISION TIME!
Have a look at the following and note which you fit into.

Then, choose which YOU typically use.

Three ways we handle our frustrations:

*Competency
*Positive Outlook
*Reactive

Competency

Competency can be displayed in different ways according to number type.

Do YOU use competency to handle your frustrations? If so, HOW do you use it?

How to handle frustration with competency

Some use competency by Being Right

They need to 'do it right'.

Being right and reforming others is a diversion when they are frustrated. Everything can get better if I do the right thing here.

The thought pattern can be, 'If I am frustrated then someone or something else is doing something wrong and it could not possibly be me because I try so hard to be right!' The underlying pattern is that the they sense the flaws of all human beings, including themselves, so contrive to fix it by doing the 'right thing'.

Of course, what is 'right' varies according to a person's value system and this is where the trouble starts. When they are doing it right they will encounter someone who does not agree that this IS in fact the right way to behave etc so they seek validation from a higher authority to defend this 'rightness' at all costs and to persuade others to do it right too.

They can be loyal and emphatic members of political parties or religious groups and honestly and wholeheartedly believe in what is right according to their perception.

DECISION TIME!

Does this sound like you? If yes, make a note of 'Being Right', if not, disregard and move to next one.

Some use competency by Being Productive

These characters display competency by efficiency and productivity to reach the goal.

They will spare no effort to strive for this success, at the cost of relationships and health, and often want others to notice that effort and drive and may want them to notice what they have achieved already in terms of monetary and material gains.

Thought patterns are a little like this, 'It means a lot to me to be well turned out and drive the best car to the best restaurant etc. Who wouldn't want that? Where's the self respect that's what I say. Everyone knows that first impressions count and that you get what you work for in this life. There is plenty of time to rest when you retire and so much to achieve in the meantime. Time is money; I can fix this.'

Of course, though, others may not join in on the validation of success being the car you drive or the watch you wear and trouble starts here with them needing to be acknowledged/admired along the way to their perceived success.

DECISION TIME!

Does this sound like you? If yes, make a note of 'Being Productive', if not, disregard and move to next one.

Some use competency by Knowing It All

They use their competency as a buffer to what they perceive as their own inadequacy. They may engross themselves in some academic, scientific, music orientated endeavour beyond the limit that other numbers would go to.

Thought patterns go a little bit like this, 'I didn't know that could happen. That will NEVER happen again because I shall be forewarned next time and I shall definitely know better.'

They contribute much to the world though this attention and intensity to acquire competency often risks other aspects of life being neglected.

DECISION TIME!
Does this sound like you? If yes, make a note of 'Knowing it all', if not, disregard and move to next section.

Positive Outlook

Positive Outlook can be displayed in different ways according to number type.

Do YOU use a positive outlook to handle your frustrations? If so, HOW do you use it?

How to handle frustration with positive outlook

Some use a positive outlook to See Themselves as Selfless

This person has the sort of philosophy that there is always someone worse off AND they are the one to help. It takes their mind off their own troubles. It is a bit like the thought processes of, 'Never you mind, help is at hand! Now, what do you need, just ask and it shall be granted. I don't wallow in my own pain when there is always someone else who is in need.'

DECISION TIME!
Does this sound like you? If yes, make a note of 'See Themselves as Selfless', if not, disregard and move to next one.

Some use a positive outlook by Good Living and Future Planning

Yes, some use a positive outlook to announce to the whole world how good they are at living life and how great life really is AND you should be doing this too!

This character thinks that there is so much joy to be had, so many experiences, such much to do, people to see, countries to explore that life is full of surprise and intrigue, colour and flavour, awe and wonder.

The only thing better than this is the future which is going to be fabulous. This outward focus of 'there could always something other than this to entertain me' distracts from what is happening now and from what adventure could be had within rather than without.

DECISION TIME!
Does this sound like you? If yes, make a note of 'Good Living and Future Planning', if not, disregard and move to next one.

Some use a positive outlook by Assuring 'It Will All Be Okay'

This is how the philosophy works in the head of this character (maybe you), 'Worse things happen at sea they say and really, it is not THAT bad. I am so very good at coping and nobody need really know how bad things are right now, because in time, everything DOES pass, though it is amazing how folks complain when they really have no right to because they have it so good really. Always look on the bright side, that's what I say.'

Does positive outlook sound like you? If yes, make a note, if not, disregard and move to next section.

DECISION TIME!
Does one of these ways of positive outlook sound like you? If yes, make a note of 'Assuring 'It Will All Be Okay'', if not, disregard and move to next one.

Reactive

Reactivity can be displayed in different ways according to number type.

Do YOU use reactivity to handle your frustrations? If so, HOW to you use it?

How to handle frustration with reactivity

Some react with an Emotionally Charged Response to Abandonment Fear

The thought processes go a little bit like this, 'I just KNEW it. This was ALWAYS going to happen. Nothing good ever happens to me and if it does it is not likely to ever happen again. That is it then. There has always been something missing, perhaps it is me, there is something wrong with me, they only pretended to like me all along. I shall never be truly happy.'

DECISION TIME!

Does this sound like you? If yes, make a note of 'Emotionally Charged Response to Abandonment Fear ', if not, disregard and move to next one.

Some react by Defending Against or Fighting It Head On

Thought processes go a bit like this, 'I know it is possible that something bad could happen right now though if I take precautions then in all likelihood I shall probably be alright. I know others think me a little over cautious but it is best to be on the safe side.'
Or…
'I shall not let myself be beaten by this. I know what could happen and it is NOT going to happen to me or anyone I love. I shall never give it the chance and I am going to do something right now to make sure that I get treated fairly and get this sorted out right now.'

DECISION TIME!

Does this sound like you? If yes, make a note of 'Defending Against or Fighting It Head On', if not, disregard and move to next one.

Some react by Domination

Any perceived threat is a call to assert dominance (sometimes a bit too quick off the mark and may get it wrong but will never admit). You puff up and shout out so you keep everyone in order. Often known as a bit over reactive, having folks say, 'I didn't mean anything by it, for goodness sake, I only asked!' Or, maybe people don't really tell you exactly how they truly feel for concern that you would 'go off on one' and you wonder why you are not told and have to find out your own way.

Or, often threat never actually occurs because you have checked everyone's opinions and beliefs beforehand and guarded against them, told them they are wrong so you don't get to the stage of being offended or hurt - angry, yes, doesn't everyone?

Does this sound like you? If yes, make a note of 'Domination', if not, disregard and move to next one.

DECISION TIME: HOW DO YOU HANDLE FRUSTRATION?

Choose one. Yes, just one.

COMPETENCY: BEING RIGHT
COMPETENCY: BEING PRODUCTIVE
COMPETENCY: BEING KNOWLEDGEABLE

POSITIVE OUTLOOK: SELFLESS
POSITIVE OUTLOOK: FUTURE PLANNING
POSITIVE OUTLOOK: IT'LL BE OKAY

REACTIVE: EMOTION OVERLOAD
REACTIVE: DEFENSIVE OR FIGHT AGAINST
REACTIVE : DOMINATION

NOTE DOWN YOUR ANSWER. You will need your answer for determining your type at the end of the Tunnel where all the answers are given.

Want to skip ahead for a sneaky peak to see the answers? ***Go to the Chapter entitled 'YOUR DECISION = YOUR NUMBER!' PAGE 235.***

7. Hornevian Type : How We Solve Conflict

Someone confronts you.

The situation is heated. It could be work or a personal relationship. The red flag is flying and someone has to come out on top. It must be someone's fault. How do you react when one on one in a heated conflict situation?

People react in one of three ways:

*Compliance
*Withdrawal
*Assertiveness

DECISION TIME!
Read through the following then make your choice.

Compliance

You comply.

Whether or not you comply by finding out what is the proper thing to do in each circumstance, looking up how to do things, asking an expert, reading the instructions, you comply.

You may patiently work with the rules already set, looking at things from all angles, working out maybe the best way to do it. You like to finish things and see them through. You are diligent, hardworking and like to please: you comply.

Compliance can be displayed in different ways according to number type.

Do YOU use compliance to solve conflict? If so, HOW do you use it?

How to solve conflict with compliance

The Right Compliance

You comply to what you KNOW to be right. This may be different to what someone else thinks, though you have spent a lifetime finding out what IS right and good and bad and your levels of discernment are pretty sharp.

You have guidelines you stick to. You may not even like it yourself sometimes, but you know you can look back and know you did the right thing, even if it means someone fell out with you over it, for example or you suffered because of the consequences.

People say things to you like, 'Why did you have to go ahead and TELL them!?' Or, 'Can't you just let this one go?' Or, 'Is it REALLY that important to you?'

So, in this confrontation, you do what is right, regardless of how that impacts on the relationship or what blame may lay at your door, or how it implicates someone else you may have preferred to protect.

DECISION TIME!
Does this sound like you? If yes, make a note of 'Right Compliance', if not, disregard and move to next one.

The Helpful Compliance

You comply to the needs of others even if you don't think it's the right thing to do, or you will be greatly inconvenienced. Someone might say something like, 'I thought you were going to the Bank today?' Or, 'Why did you agree to give them a lift when I thought we were going to have a drink?' Or, '..but YOU wanted to go to the Florida, didn't you, not skiing?'

You put yourself out, you genuinely like others, though you like them a bit more than you will ever like yourself, until the time comes when they overlook you or favour someone instead of you after all you've done for them.

So, in this confrontation, you do what you think is best for the other person, graciously apologising or flattering them and making them feel better, telling them how much you admire them or what a wonderful person they really are.

You may gladly take the blame. You do this to keep the relationship sweet, to keep them liking you even if you somehow suffer in the meantime. You worry how you can make them feel better - you hate to see people cry, forgetting the times they may have upset you.

DECISION TIME!

Does this sound like you? If yes, make a note of 'Helpful Compliance', if not, disregard and move to next one.

The Safe Compliance

You comply by ingratiating yourself with others because you don't want to do this alone. It could be that this conflict may result in your job being in jeopardy and you could be out of work and that would be horrendous.

It may be that this conflict could mean you are ostracised, cast out from the group as you must be the only one who feels this way so standing strong for what you believe in becomes less important than making a fuss when you are the only one who feels this way.

It tears you apart to not back up your friend in a conflict but your support is demonstrated more in trying to assure them of your allegiance in other ways rather than pitting yourself against the larger group.

So, in this confrontation, you do everything you can to remain secure in your job, relationship, club, family, because you don't want to be out in the cold. You may not like it, though you convince yourself it is best to comply with the greater power, to not make too much of a fuss about this.

Does compliance sound like you? If yes, make a note, if not, disregard and move to next section.

DECISION TIME!

Does this sound like you? If yes, make a note of 'Safe Compliance', if not, disregard and move to next one.

Withdraw

Withdrawing can be done differently according to number type.

You contemplate life deeply. You strive to understand yourself and others and you ask the question 'why?' a lot, even if it is just in your own head.

Left to your own devices, you come up with new and interesting ways to do things. You innovate. To others you seem 'withdrawn' but there is lots going on within you.

Like the proverbial swan, looking calm on the outside but legs going like the clappers under the surface, you are working it all out on a deeper level.

You are a good listening and put up with a lot that maybe you do not agree with, though why share your opinion if it is going to fall on deaf ears or be challenged continually? For this, you are known to bring stability and a calmness to a situation.

You help others understand, if they take the time to understand you.

DECISION TIME!

Do YOU withdraw to solve conflict? If so, HOW do you withdraw?

How to solve conflict by withdrawing

Withdraw to Inner Emotional Realm

The thought processes of this character go something like this.

'The world is flawed - there is something wrong, many things wrong and I'm just trying to get by the best I can within it. I reinterpret things, I dream of a better place, a better circumstance, just better.

I can reproduce things better than they appear in reality and my inner landscape is a far nicer place to be.'

In one to one conflict, you do what you've got to do, though don't expect me to do or say what you expect. You don't know me. I don't need to prove myself to you. I am not likely to tell you how I truly feel because you don't have the capacity to understand anyway.

Yes, whatever, just let me withdraw to imaginary constructs and inner emotions and let me be.

DECISION TIME!

Does this sound like you? If yes, make a note of 'Inner Emotional Realm', if not, disregard and move to next one.

Withdraw to The Mental Realm

The thought processes go like this. 'There must be something here I am missing. I'm sure that I can fix this if I can just find out enough. I accept that there is a gap, a piece of knowledge that has escaped me up until now. How could that be? I had best hop to and gen up on this and be better than I am. Next time... no this will never happen again, because next time I shall know better, I shall BE better. I didn't see this one coming. Never mind, I'll sort it out. Now, where shall I begin.

In one to one confrontation these characters are gracious and non-confrontational. They ask, 'Give me some time to figure this one out. I need time to think it through then I shall get back to you. Leave it with me, okay?'

DECISION TIME!
Does this sound like you? If yes, make a note of 'Mental Realm', if not, disregard and move to next one.

Withdraw by Invisibility Cloaking

These are the people who are there, but not really present. They are hovering on the periphery, finding a way to disassociate. They experience conflict as a physical disturbance deep inside the core of their Being and feel intense discomfort.

They will be sitting right there with the group and somehow, in matters where they disagree or dislike what is happening, they blend into the background. You will wonder why they aren't in the group wedding photograph or you will suddenly think of them and have to seek them out in a gathering. They are not 'making their presence known' in discussions unless they are passionate about the topic and then they make powerful contributions, though these times are few and far between.

They zone out, convince themselves that whatever occurred to them to object to isn't really a big deal as almost immediately they see the conflict from the other's point of view and in making excuses for them, understand too readily and almost become the other.

So, in this matter of one to one conflict they just want you to shut up and go away and leave them alone. They may say or do anything to get you to stop, even if it means they take blame upon themselves that isn't theirs. They implode on the inside to such a degree they shall freeze up and go quiet and just wonder why on earth you are being so mean, rather than process what you are trying to communicate.

DECISION TIME!

Does withdrawing sound like you? If yes, make a note of 'Invisibility Cloaking', if not, disregard and move to next section.

Assertive

Assertiveness can be done differently according to number type.

You are perceived as confident, even daring.

You can be relied upon to take charge when no one else seems to know what on earth needs to be done. You know. It is glaringly obvious and you cannot understand the laziness of others to not jump into action.

You stand up, you stand out, you speak up either for yourself or for the injustices of others. You thrive on interaction, particularly in matters when there are disagreements flying around. There is an energy vibe within conflict that ignites your soul. Others are lit up by your boldness, your courage, your strategic action plans that you shamelessly share with others.

Do YOU solve conflict by being assertive? If so, HOW do you assert yourself?

How to solve conflict by asserting yourself

Assertion of Entitlement

This assertion is contained within the framework of advancing self-interest, or towards accumulating status or ownership. For example, there must be a personal advantage here for me and I feel I have earned the right to this advantage, by working hard or by rights of inheritance. I shall seek to grasp the prize if presented, or if the threat of losing it to another manifests.

This is not an asserting of Will that spills over into the wider world, though it may present itself if close loved ones are threatened. Focus is on improving one's condition and preserving and furthering image.

Entitlement is born of true hope. It dictates that what is wanted can ultimately be possessed and that events will turn out for the best for them, so conflict comes as a shock to challenge this perception.

The thought processes of this character go a little bit like this... 'This is my world, this is my life which I have worked hard for/have the right to - and if you are going to take something away from me or back me into a corner then watch out.

'You shall not take anything away from me that I have earned the right to have. I shall not be the loser here and I refuse to endure condemnation so I shall find a way to deflect, detract and most probably will joke or charm my way out of this one.

'I am going to react; I am going to do something here and I am quick witted enough to get away with murder so why fight the hard way?'

Assertion tends to be very strategic and applied to advance their position. So, in this matter of head to head conflict I shall escape, I shall duck and dive and beguile and somehow turn it into what you think is a win win situation. I may let you believe that you have won - as long as it goes my way.

So, in this matter of conflict, 'eyes on the prize' is the saying that applies here!

DECISION TIME!
Does this sound like you? If yes, make a note of 'Assertion of Entitlement', if not, disregard and move to next one.

Assertion of Desire

This assertion is born of the energy of desire, fancy, an enhancement of experience, to elevate one's enjoyment of life.

'I may not have all the facts at my fingertips, though I want this so much that my pure enthusiasm and belief will win through. What I may lack in qualification I more than make up for in verve and I shall put the effort in and prove myself more than anyone else and you know that's right.'

The other party may get swept away on the energy exuded by this character and begin to doubt their own opposition.

Or, in matters of romance, 'I will have you, oh yes, you will be mine. I will do whatever it takes and not take no for an answer, yes indeed I will. I've set my sights on you and you cannot help but give in to my affections, until maybe I go off the idea.'

So, in this matter of conflict, 'pleasure at all costs' is the saying that applies here!

DECISION TIME!
Does this sound like you? If yes, make a note of 'Assertion of Desire', if not, disregard and move to next one.

Assertion of Strength

This assertion may begin with assertion of strength for the self, to prevent or remedy injustice thrust upon the individual, though spreads to encompass the justices of the entire world.

Feeling a sense of justice on behalf of the weaker, the fragile and innocent this character will put right those who would seek to take advantage. For example, there must be a wider agenda here than me asserting myself merely for selfish endeavor. You do not even have to engage me in conflict, for I will initiate that conflict if I perceive some wrongdoing of me, my loved ones or even strangers that are 'picked on' by you.

Thought processes of this character go a little bit like this, 'Displays of conflict towards me mean that you think you are somehow better than me.

'Bring it on, let's work this out and do not expect me to give in or let you think that I am in the one in the wrong here.

'I am not weak. Make no mistake. I shall stand up for myself and those I choose to protect. How dare you challenge me before you have all the facts. I shall put you right. Not only that, I shall tell the world how wrong you are to assert yourself toward me.

'You may think you are stronger than me because you think you have more money, more status or more influence than me, though I shall find where the chinks in your armor are. I am older/younger/wiser/more honest/more powerful than you. I will find a way to convince myself that this is a situation where somehow, I am stronger.'

You note what result you want from this and you go get it. This is going to be resolved and it will be resolved now, come hell or high water. Failure is not an option. 'Just who do they think they are?' It can be done quietly or it can be done loudly but, it WILL be done. So, in this one to one confrontation, you will do what you need to in order to win and will come out of the situation having asserted dominance. Maybe the other party gives in at the time because of the sheer force of your energetic will - though they may find another way to redress the balance later.

DECISION TIME!

Does this sound like you? If yes, make a note of 'Assertion of Strength', if not, disregard and move to next one.

DECISION TIME: HOW DO YOU SOLVE CONFLICT?

Choose one.

THE RIGHT COMPLIANCE
THE HELPFUL COMPLIANCE
THE SAFE COMPLIANCE

WITHDRAW TO INNER REALM
WITHDRAW TO MENTAL REALM
WITHDRAW TO INVISIBILITY

ASSERTION OF ENTITLEMENT
ASSERTION OF DESIRE
ASSERTION OF STRENGTH

NOTE DOWN YOUR ANSWER. You will need your answer for determining your type at the end of the Tunnel where all the answers are given.

Want to skip ahead for a sneaky peak to see the answers? ***Go to the Chapter entitled 'YOUR DECISION = YOUR NUMBER!' PAGE 235.***

8. Focus of Attention – Where Our Energy Naturally Gravitates To

External or Internal

Do not confuse this with being introvert or extrovert. This is where your attention naturally gravitates. One person's 'selfish' is another person's 'self reference' and just a normal case of having to look out for oneself, for instance. One person's 'shy' is another's 'me time' and maybe they just don't want to go out to play right now! So, you will be usually focused on yourself or on others, there is no right or wrong. Then you can take it a bit further.

Read through the next section and note down which MOSTLY relates to you and your usual pattern in everyday life and where you tend to put the most energy.

External

What is wrong with others and how should this be made better?

What does this other person need and how can I adjust myself/what I'm doing to accommodate them?

What is the goal here and how do I win through? How can I be better than I am right now, how can I be the best I can be at this? How am I doing, what do others think of me, am I wearing the right clothes, exuding the right image here? What's the next step for me?

How can this get better? Well, okay, that didn't work out as well as I expected, though this next thing is going to solve that, I can quickly readjust and change the goal because this is bound to work out better than that other thing anyway. I don't know why I wasted my time, because now I really know what to do. It's going to be more enjoyable and I'm really looking forward to it, aren't you? Can't you see how much better life could be? Yes! Cheer up! Come on!

Where is the power? Who has it and are they friend or foe? I really don't know what is going on over there and I need to test out the waters, to see who has my back and who might be a problem. Let's push a little here and there to see how the land lies, because it is not always as you expect.

I was going to do this today though I didn't realise that we needed this so I'll just readjust things slightly so I can make sure that gets done and if I just do this other thing, before doing the thing that I wanted to do then life will be a little bit better because that will stop this or that happening and we are going to need that later and that will stop any arguments from happening. So and so is going to be so pleased when I've done this and I love to see them happy. Oh and I just noticed as I was doing that thing that this other thing needs doing to and now I've totally forgotten what I WAS going to do, oh yes I remember though I can do that thing I was going to do anytime really and it wasn't that important anyway and to be honest I'm quite tired out now.

DECISION TIME!

Does this sound like you? If yes, make a note of one of the 6 bold headings, if not, disregard and move to next one.

Internal

Things used to be so much better than this. I don't know what I did wrong or what went wrong but I DO remember things being so much better. Maybe it's me. If only I wasn't so different and could fit in better though when I think about it I'm not sure what I really want anyway. I thought I wanted this or that but I really don't know how to make myself happy. Folks tell me to find an interest, to do something I enjoy but what do they know, it's so much easier for them isn't it.

There is still much to figure out and so much to contemplate I don't know how people find time to indulge their feelings, it is really just a question of working out how life works and putting your energy into focusing on what is best for you and those you care about, isn't it? It really is never enough though, there is also more to explore and to investigate and if I am going to go and do this thing I had better make sure I make the best choice and find out about it first.

I am a bit of a worrier, though there is lots to worry about isn't there? So much can go wrong and it is good to be prepared. I know I can be guilty of a bit of a disconnect from intensity of feeling from time to time and I think instead to avoid overwhelm when someone becomes a bit demanding. I wonder what is the next thing the world wants from me. I can think my way out of this and ahead of time to figure life out and guard against any potential things going wrong. I can look at the map, investigate the situation, understand it so well that nothing will take me by surprise, yes. That is how I shall do it.

DECISION TIME!

Does this sound like you? If yes, make a note of one of the 3 bold headings.

DECISION TIME: WHERE IS YOUR FOCUS OF ATTENTION?

So, choose one.

EXTERNAL: WHAT IS WRONG?
EXTERNAL: WHAT DOES THIS OTHER PERSON NEED?
EXTERNAL: WHAT IS THE GOAL HERE?

EXTERNAL: HOW CAN THIS GET BETTER?
EXTERNAL: WHERE IS THE POWER?
EXTERNAL: I WAS GOING TO DO THIS...

INTERNAL: THINGS USED TO BE SO MUCH BETTER
INTERNAL: THERE IS STILL SO MUCH TO FIGURE OUT
INTERNAL: I AM A BIT OF A WORRIER

NOTE DOWN YOUR ANSWER. You will need your answer for determining your type at the end of the Tunnel where all the answers are given.

Want to skip ahead for a sneaky peak to see the answers? ***Go to the Chapter entitled 'YOUR DECISION = YOUR NUMBER!' PAGE 235.***

9.Find Your Virtue

The virtue for each type is what is lacking or needed to compensate for the corresponding sin/passion.

It dissolves the emotional demands of the passion.

Below is one interpretation of how these virtues apply to each Enneagram personality type.

The rhymes and reasons may escape us, though those patterns are there and will keep occurring until we make some sort of inner advancement, with these virtues being what we need to develop. Furthermore, it seems we chose to have these challenges – on some level of our Being.

This may be the trickiest section for you. What do you think you need to soothe your angst I wonder. Realise that everything is a reflection - so if you are concerned about being corrupt, then corruption in the world drives you up the wall. What do you think you would need to calm this focus for you? Now, that is all the clues I am giving.

Serenity

Serenity arises when the world is accepted as it is. Critical anger finds no target when the world is not in need of being corrected.

Humility

Humility arises when the self is seen as no more or less important than others. The self-inflation of pride gives way when you realise you're not as indispensable as imagined.

Truthfulness

Truthfulness arises when the true self is accepted. The packaging and selling of oneself becomes unnecessary when there is no reason for deceitful appearances.

Equanimity

Equanimity arises when you see both your positive and negatives equally. The half-truth of envy loses its validity when you stop comparing the positives of others with the negatives of the self.

Detachment

Detachment from isolation arises when you learn the world is better understood by participating in it rather than learning about it from the periphery. The desperate need for one's own space and time often makes one less prepared to live in the world not more. In this context, one needs to learn to detach from one's own sense of detachment from others and the world and allow integration.

Courage

Courage arises when negative possibilities are seen as a product of the mind and not reality. Action against or away from fear becomes irrelevant when the fear is seen as self-created.

Sobriety

Sobriety arises when it's realized that a more meaningful and deeper experience of life is missed when it's superficially sampled. Gluttony of the mind racing through life pursues a quantity of life forsaking a quality of life.

Innocence

Innocence arises when the more subtle sensations and emotions are allowed to surface. Excesses and intensity of experience are needed only when one is unable to appreciate or experience the subtleties of life.

Right Action

Right action allows one to live and pursue one's personal goals and desires. Laziness or inertia that depends on others for direction leads to a life not fully lived for oneself.

DECISION TIME: SO WHAT IS YOUR VIRTUE?

SERENITY

HUMILITY

TRUTHFULNESS

EQUANIMITY

DETACHMENT

COURAGE

SOBRIETY

INNOCENCE

RIGHT ACTION

NOTE DOWN YOUR ANSWER. You will need your answer for determining your type at the end of the Tunnel where all the answers are given.

Want to skip ahead for a sneaky peak to see the answers? ***Go to the Chapter entitled 'YOUR DECISION = YOUR NUMBER!' PAGE 235.***

10.Find Your Fear

What is your fear?

Right, let's get this over with: we all have ALL of these fears to some degree. What I want you to do here is to pick out which is your BIGGEST fear, which rises to the surface in its prominence for you - this will give you a big clue to your ultimate number type.

Another thing that is important for me to say here is that these fears, though seeming to be very, very real, are perceptions of reality and exposing them to ourselves is the real basis of positive change. They get reflected outside of ourselves and become the lens that we perceive the world through, for our own protection.

The fear of being evil or corrupt

In striving to be morally upstanding and virtuous in the face of a corrupt world this pervasive, underlying fear is that we ourselves are corrupt.

We know that we all are, to some degree, but this character type is really disturbed by the fact that they are and seeks to be as good or 'right' as they possibly can, doing the right things, behaving the right way, following the structures and rules that promise rewards to those that do things the correct way.

So, if I am this type, I then get annoyed (though we don't want to admit it and so cloak it to ourselves because angry people are not good people) about doing all the right things and then getting overlooked for promotion, or having our loved one leave us, or being done down by a tradesman or short changed by a store.

The unexpressed anger turns to resentment.

Having a profound sense of integrity, I am constantly aiming to move away from corruption and 'being bad' towards virtue, or the greater good.

This gets reflected out to the world as I have a keen eye for wrongdoings in society and the world at large and it is then safe for me to be enraged by some news article or event that is openly deemed to be 'bad' and can discuss it safely with others.

DECISION TIME!
Does this sound like you? If yes, make a note of 'being evil or corrupt', if not, disregard and move to next one.

.

The fear of being unloved or unwanted by others

These folks love to be loved and wanted by those around them. Yes, who doesn't? However, for these people, this is a big thing for them - massive.

Their pervasive, underlying fear is that they are NOT loveable and they must therefore help others in order to earn their love.

They must be worthy of care and love from others. It is tricky for these folks to merely accept that they ARE loved and they are almost looking for chinks in the armour of the love bestowed on them.

Not everyone that loves you is going to behave in a loving way one hundred percent of the time they are with you and if I were this character type, then I would be wary of those times when someone didn't seem to like me much and I would seek to 'solve' this by being extra loving towards them.

I would be constantly aiming to move away from being unwanted and towards relationships that give some loving and caregiving back to me and be really perplexed if it was not returned.

This gets reflected out to the world as I have a keen interest in being loved and seek it out at all costs.

DECISION TIME!
Does this sound like you? If yes, make a note of 'being unloved or unwanted', if not, disregard and move to next one.

The fear of being worthless
We strive to achieve success within our families, our jobs and our community because we believe it to be a measure of our own worth.
Our pervasive, underlying fear is that we are inherently worthless and undesirable. However, our achievements save us, letting us know that we ARE worthwhile and a worthy member of the human race.

If I were this character, I would therefore accomplish as much as possible in order to be desired and accepted by others.

I am constantly aiming to move away from worthlessness and towards impressive achievements that will earn me respect and admiration of others.

This gets reflected out to the world as I have a keen interest in the worth of things and people and don't want to waste my time pursing things without value.

DECISION TIME!
Does this sound like you? If yes, make a note of 'being worthless', if not, disregard and move to next one.

The fear of not being special

These people strive to prove their uniqueness and individuality. Their pervasive, underlying fear is that they would be worthless and unlovable if they were average, which must be avoided at all costs. They are often envious of others or what others have and even of their past or future selves, remembering when things were better, or hoping that at some point in the future things will greatly improve.

Their own significance hinges on how different they are from others. They are constantly aiming to move away from normalcy and towards expressions of intensity and being a true individual.

This is reflected from me out into the world as there being 'something missing'. There is something inherently wrong in the world, just like secretly I think there must have been something wrong with me.

DECISION TIME!

Does this sound like you? If yes, make a note of 'not being special', if not, disregard and move to next one.

The fear of being useless or incapable.

These are the ones who strive to become as knowledgeable and competent as possible in all of the things they do. From balancing the books to washing their car or making a pizza, knowledge and expertise is important.

Their pervasive, underlying fear is of being useless, overwhelmed and incapable of dealing with the world around them which is a scary place and having expertise will be a good defense against those dangers.

Therefore, they must not only learn as much as they can about something, they must become its master so they can reassure themselves and those they love, that they are competent and capable.

They are constantly aiming to move away from ignorance and towards knowledge and understanding.

DECISION TIME!
Does this sound like you? If yes, make a note of 'being useless or incapable', if not, disregard and move to next one.

The fear of being without support or guidance.

These folks strive to bond with likeminded others to find support and guidance from them. Their pervasive, underlying fear is that they are incapable of making it alone, seeking out as much support and direction from others as possible. It's not that we will take the advice, but we need to hear it.

They are constantly aiming to move away from isolation and towards structure, security and the guidance of others or groups and philosophies which promise to give them what they need. This can be work, social groups, religious gatherings, weight clubs, orchestras, in fact any collectives which provide inclusion and acceptance for them.

This lack of support for oneself gets reflected out into the world as there must be something or someone out there who can support me, show me the way, give me the guidance I need - maybe government benefit or a reliable job, a decent hardworking partner or religious order that must know how to see to my needs and look after me because I fear I might not know how to do that for myself.

DECISION TIME!

Does this sound like you? If yes, make a note of 'being without support or guidance', if not, disregard and move to next one.

The fear of being restricted and in pain

These are the ones who have outlandish (as others think them to be) desires and seek to satisfy themselves at every opportunity. Their pervasive, underlying fear is that their needs and desires will never be met by others, and so they must go and pursue them independently.

They are constantly aiming to move away from pain, sadness and confinement and towards independence, happiness and fulfilment of somewhat fanciful ideas.

The future is always going to be better and there's no point in dwelling on the miseries of life when the grass is definitely greener and more wonderful than now.

If I were this character I would cover my disappointment well, because in idealising the next best thing that is to come it can never live up to the dream I have made it to be.

This lack of adventuring and inability to find fulfilment in any given moment, gets reflected out into the world as a constant seeking of future pleasure as this thing happening right here is never enough - not happy enough, not tasty enough, not sensational enough, never enough.

DECISION TIME!
Does this sound like you? If yes, make a note of 'being restricted and in pain', if not, disregard and move to next one.

The fear of being hurt or controlled by others

These characters strive to be strong, independent and self-directed. Their pervasive, underlying fear is of being violated, betrayed or controlled by anyone else.

They are constantly aiming to move away from uncertain limitations and toward self-sufficiency and power.

If I were this character I would be entering into most situations asking myself who has the power here and what can I do with it to wield it to my advantage. These folks don't like weakness, though they will fight to the death to defend the genuinely disadvantaged and how dare you seek to dominate them for you will encounter their wrath.

Defender of the innocent and attacker of injustice, I shall pounce on your shilly shallowing and indecision and force you into a corner.

This fear of being hurt and controlled by another gets reflected out into the world as having to attack first and ask questions later as the world is out to get you.

DECISION TIME!

Does this sound like you? If yes, make a note of 'being hurt or controlled by others', if not, disregard and move to next one.

The fear of separation and loss

These characters strive to maintain peace and harmony both internally and externally.

Their pervasive, underlying fear is that they will become disconnected from others and cast out of the world around them.

They seek harmony at (almost) all costs, certainly they give in readily to the demands of others unless they are really, really, moved to oppose and then, stand well back as hidden strengths take the unaware by surprise.

They are constantly moving away from conflict and pain and towards peace, stability and harmony.

Their feelings of loss and separation they are constantly experiencing on the inside are reflected outwardly by strident attempts to keep everyone together and getting along with each other.

The message they heard was 'nobody cares'.

DECISION TIME!

Does this sound like you? If yes, make a note of 'separation and loss'.

DECISION TIME: WHAT IS YOUR FEAR?

BEING EVIL OR CORRUPT

BEING UNWANTED OR UNLOVED

BEING WORTHLESS OR WITHOUT VALUE

BEING NOT SPECIAL

BEING INCAPABLE OR INCOMPETENT

BEING UNSUPPORTED OR WITHOUT GUIDANCE

BEING TRAPPED OR IN PAIN

BEING HURT OR CONTROLLED

BEING SEPARATED OR FEELING LOSS

NOTE DOWN YOUR ANSWER. You will need your answer for determining your type at the end of the Tunnel where all the answers are given.

Want to skip ahead for a sneaky peak to see the answers? ***Go to the Chapter entitled 'YOUR DECISION = YOUR NUMBER!' PAGE 235.***

YOUR DECISION = YOUR NUMBER!

So here we are! Well done. Now that you have all your answers to the previous sections, it is now time to marry those up with the number types that relate to each answer. As you go through, notice what number type this section gives for the answers that you have given to verify your number type. It is the majority that wins, so just see how many times a particular number appears in your answers to give you your typing.

ANSWER: DECISION TIME: WHICH TRIAD ARE YOU?

GUT PEOPLE ARE
ANSWER: 8/9/1

HEART PEOPLE ARE
ANSWER: 2/3/4

HEAD PEOPLE ARE
ANSWER: 5/6/7

ANSWER: DECISION TIME: WHAT IS YOUR FIXATION?

RESENTMENT
ANSWER:1

FLATTERY
ANSWER:2

VANITY
ANSWER:3

MELANCHOLY
ANSWER:4

HOARDING
ANSWER:5

COWARDICE
ANSWER:6

PLANNING
ANSWER:7

VENGEANCE
ANSWER:8

INDOLENCE
ANSWER:9

ANSWER: DECISION TIME: WHAT IS YOUR TRAP?

PERFECTION
ANSWER:1

FREEDOM

ANSWER:2

EFFICIENCY
ANSWER:3

AUTHENTICITY
ANSWER:4

OBSERVATION
ANSWER:5

SECURITY
ANSWER:6

IDEALISM
ANSWER:7

JUSTICE
ANSWER:8

SEEKING
ANSWER:9

ANSWER: DECISION TIME: WHAT IS YOUR SIN?

ANGER
ANSWER:1

PRIDE
ANSWER:2

DECEIT
ANSWER:3

ENVY
ANSWER:4

AVARICE
ANSWER:5

FEAR
ANSWER:6

GLUTTONY
ANSWER:7

EXCESS
ANSWER:8

LAZINESS
ANSWER:9

ANSWER: DECISION TIME: WHAT IS YOUR WOUND?

THINKING I'M EVIL OR CORRUPT
ANSWER:1

THINKING I'M UNWANTED OR UNLOVED
ANSWER:2

THINKING I'M WORTHLESS OR WITHOUT VALUE
ANSWER:3

THINKING I'M NOT SPECIAL
ANSWER:4

THINKING I'M INCAPABLE OR INCOMPETENT
ANSWER:5

THINKING I'M UNSUPPORTED OR WITHOUT GUIDANCE
ANSWER:6

THINKING I'M TRAPPED OR IN PAIN
ANSWER:7

THINKING I'M HURT OR CONTROLLED
ANSWER:8

THINKING I'M SEPARATED OR FEELING LOSS
ANSWER:9

ANSWER: DECISION TIME: HOW DO YOU HANDLE FRUSTRATION?

COMPETENCY: BEING RIGHT
ANSWER: 1

COMPETENCY: BEING PRODUCTIVE
ANSWER: 3

COMPETENCY: BEING KNOWLEDGEABLE
ANSWER: 5

POSITIVE OUTLOOK: SELFLESS
ANSWER: 2

POSITIVE OUTLOOK: FUTURE PLANNING
ANSWER: 7

POSITIVE OUTLOOK: IT'LL BE OKAY
ANSWER: 9

REACTIVE: EMOTION OVERLOAD
ANSWER: 4

REACTIVE: DEFENSIVE OR FIGHT AGAINST
ANSWER: 6

REACTIVE: DOMINATION
ANSWER: 8

ANSWER: DECISION TIME: HOW DO YOU SOLVE CONFLICT?

THE RIGHT COMPLIANCE

ANSWER:1

THE HELPFUL COMPLIANCE
ANSWER:2

THE SAFE COMPLIANCE
ANSWER:6

WITHDRAW TO INNER REALM
ANSWER:4

WITHDRAW TO MENTAL REALM
ANSWER:5

WITHDRAW TO INVISIBILITY
ANSWER:9

ASSERTION OF ENTITLEMENT
ANSWER:3

ASSERTION OF DESIRE
ANSWER:7

ASSERTION OF STRENGTH
ANSWER:8

ANSWER: DECISION TIME: WHERE IS YOUR FOCUS OF ATTENTION?

EXTERNAL: WHAT IS WRONG?
ANSWER:1

EXTERNAL: WHAT DOES THIS OTHER PERSON NEED?
ANSWER:2

EXTERNAL: WHAT IS THE GOAL HERE?
ANSWER:3

EXTERNAL: HOW CAN THIS GET BETTER?
ANSWER:7

EXTERNAL: WHERE IS THE POWER?
ANSWER:8

EXTERNAL: I WAS GOING TO DO THIS...
ANSWER:9

INTERNAL: THINGS USED TO BE SO MUCH BETTER
ANSWER:4

INTERNAL: THERE IS STILL SO MUCH TO FIGURE OUT
ANSWER:5

INTERNAL: I AM A BIT OF A WORRIER
ANSWER:6

ANSWER: DECISION TIME: SO WHAT IS YOUR VIRTUE?

SERENITY
ANSWER:1

HUMILITY
ANSWER:2

TRUTHFULNESS
ANSWER:3

EQUANIMITY
ANSWER:4

DETACHMENT
ANSWER:5

COURAGE
ANSWER:6

SOBRIETY
ANSWER:7

INNOCENCE
ANSWER:8

RIGHT ACTION
ANSWER:9

ANSWER: DECISION TIME: WHAT IS YOUR FEAR?

BEING EVIL OR CORRUPT
ANSWER:1

BEING UNWANTED OR UNLOVED
ANSWER:2

BEING WORTHLESS OR WITHOUT VALUE
ANSWER:3

BEING NOT SPECIAL
ANSWER:4

BEING INCAPABLE OR INCOMPETENT
ANSWER:5

BEING UNSUPPORTED OR WITHOUT GUIDANCE
ANSWER:6

BEING TRAPPED OR IN PAIN
ANSWER:7

BEING HURT OR CONTROLLED
ANSWER:8

BEING SEPARATED OR FEELING LOSS
ANSWER:9

Congratulations!
Looking through your list of answers you should now have a number that has appeared more times than the rest.

It is highly likely that this is your Kitching Whittaker Enneagram Type, especially if it also matches the number you received upon completing the Adventure.

You can now read the rest of the book specifically focusing on the information that applies to your Type.

Welcome to you.

The Antidotes to Illusions and Delusions

So, each Trap has its corresponding 'Holy Idea' The nine Holy Ideas are all representations of the same ONE reality.

Each highlights a particular facet of our perception. This lens that we look through, perceiving reality through its colour, its shape, its formulaic structure, gives rise to delusion.

Yes, time to realise we are all deluded!   If you ever hear a spiritual person telling you your life is but an illusion of your own creation, this is what they are talking about.

Learning to experiment with the acceptance of our own particular delusion is essential to our further understanding of the Enneagram. This is the real road to freedom, rather than analysing our personality trait and arriving at a confining, defining, seemingly immovable numbered category. That is like recognising you are in prison and just accepting you are never going to be given the key or the escape plan.

There IS a key, there is a method of charting your great escape!

More importantly, knowing your own delusions gives rise to understanding all of the others, because you wouldn't have yours if it weren't for your interactions with others anyway.

It is by mixing with everyone else's behaviours and motivations and manipulations that you react in certain ways at certain times, with certain personalities.

You already know that you behave differently according to the circumstances you find yourself in and in acknowledgement of those that happen to be around you at the time, don't you? You respond differently at work to how you would at home. You act differently with the window salesman to how you behave with the local vicar, maybe.

Practical Advice

So many of us have problems with lack. This can manifest as lack of money, lack of security, lack of love, lack of company, lack of interest/adventure, lack of control over behaviour/events etc.

Lack is a factor at the core of our personality. How we fill that hole, how we compensate for that lack is a key issue to determining our prison – and to chart our escape.

It's Alright for YOU!

Everything is truly a perception. Others may think you have it all sorted Oh, they might say, it's easy for you. You don't have my problems. Money? Money is easy to come by, but health, well that's another matter. You can always get more money but you will never get another body! Yes, health is an issue, a REAL issue!

Health? That's easy, just stop drinking yourself to death, get some exercise and get off your backside, health is easy, it just happens when you stop thwarting it. Now MONEY, that's the big issue, really, money is a REAL problem!

Relationships? Relationships are two-a-penny, what you REALLY need is good solid investments and there is no better investment than property... always make sure you keep the house!

NLP enthusiasts have two questions they advise you ask when this sort of stuff raises its head: is it true/is it useful? This used to drive me crazy. Nowadays I find myself asking these questions of others. When someone complains they have 'no money', for example, I ask if it is true.

Often the answer is, 'well, you know what I mean', to which I reply, 'no', and they then either explains more lucidly or walk away in a huff!

Each moan, each irritation, each observation needs to be examined and explored, rather than assumed to be true because the unconscious mind TAKES YOU LITERALLY. It is no fool, though it does accept, by the way, that if you go around saying sorry to people when it is not your fault, for example, that you are consistently to blame and you may get to the state of mind where you feel nothing you ever do is right. In fact it is the very moans and irritations; the arguments we have with the world, that can lead us to our numbered type.

We all have our upsets, though follow them back to the source and like a trail of breadcrumbs, you find your way to the truth.

The 9s, for example, who's Holy Truth is Love, experience the absence of it, the lack of it, acutely. All numbers do, of course, but 9s are especially sensitive to it. It is as if they are looking through the lens of 'the lack of love'. When dissolving, the 9 will inwardly think, 'see, I KNEW it, I KNEW they never really loved me!'

When looking at our lives from a higher, more detached perspective (Hypnotherapists call it the 'Observer Self', if they go with the Hilgard Model) then you realise that everything influences everything else and we cannot be responsible for all that occurs, though we CAN witness our own behaviours and responses to that influence and experiment with a different behaviour.

As long as we keep our grip on trying to control things to 'go our way' then we are striving toward an ego determined outcome and continue to suffer.

Therefore, I urge that it is the frustrations and the fear of your particular type that will give you the most information about yourself and your own particular way forward.

The Antidote to Your Trap:

So, by now you already know SO very much about yourself, particularly to know your trap - so here you have the key to unlock your prison and escape being trapped in the future.

While the individual will tend to focus on a limited, self-centered idea, ie the Fixations and Traps which put us in prison, the holy idea expands the concept to a more universal context. So, bearing in mind that now you know what your trap is, here is your antidote. Use it as a mantra to live by as it will make your life a whole lot easier.

The Antidote to Perfection

Type 1: Perfection comes from an effort to live up to a very personalised idea of perfection (disguised as 'perfection for all')

Seek perfection in the flawed and the imperfect

Holy perfection aligns with a more universal sense of perfection where the individual sense of perfection need not be forced upon the world.

The Antidote to Freedom

Type 2: This is a freedom which creates a sense of being needed by attending to the needs of others instead of one's own needs; in a sense 'freeing' you of the obligation to see to your own self.

Find joy in helping because helping helps you feel joy!

Holy Will attends to the needs of others within reason (not over-extending oneself, or looking after others to one's detriment). The willpower is utilised to balance helping others with helping oneself and helping without having the need to be loved or even appreciated in return.

The Antidote to Efficiency

Type 3: Efficiency in the performance of task and accomplishment is used to measure one's self-worth and judge oneself against some impossible standard.

Know when enough is enough

Holy law points to how the universal laws flow; to the natural order of things where one doesn't need to over perform in order to prove one's worth.

The Antidote to Authenticity

Type 4: This trap seeks an authentic sense of self by cultivating an emotional uniqueness that stands apart from others.

Celebrate the specialness of every human being

Holy origin points to a more inherent unfolding of one's own uniqueness in the universe without having to overtly distinguish oneself.

The Antidote to Observation

Type 5: As observation requires a detachment from or non-involvement with the world in order to objectively understand it, one separates oneself from oneself.

Become an active part of it all to contribute and co-create.

Holy omniscience is knowledge of the world through participation and experience in it rather than watching from the sidelines in the hope of understanding it before jumping in.

The Antidote to Security

Type 6: Security pursues certainty through questioning and doubting what the self and others are thinking.

Be courageous enough to be certain in an uncertain world.

Holy strength draws from a belief that the universe eventually works itself to a resolution and trust in that means moving forward even in uncertainty.

The Antidote to Idealism

Type 7: Idealism reframes the pains of reality into something more appealing.

Appreciate that your pains make up who you are and there is adventure in meeting life's challenges.

Holy wisdom experiences a more complete reality by embracing both the positive and negative instead of escaping into transitory pleasures.

The Antidote to Justice

Type 8: The trap of justice attempts to balance the scales according to a personal sense of fairness justice based solely on one's own point of view.

Innocently recognise everyone has their own truth.

Holy truth sees the grey of a more universal truth which lies between the black and white absolutes of the individual's truth.

The Antidote to Indolence

Type 9: The indolence trap seeks to merge and blend with the environment around oneself as a result of one's own sense of personal insignificance.

Know that all people are wonderful and worthy of love and that YOU are a people too.

Holy love holds that every being in the universe has value and significance both as part of something greater and as an individual.

WHAT IS YOUR ANTIDOTE?

It is a good idea to make a note of your antidote to your trap, just so that you have a constant awareness of what you are working on freeing yourself from.

PERFECTON: Seek perfection in the flawed and the imperfect

FREEDOM: Find joy in helping because helping helps you feel joy!

EFFICIENCY: Know when enough is enough

AUTHENTICITY: Celebrate the specialness of every human being

OBSERVATION: Become an active part of it all to contribute and co-create.

SECURITY: Be courageous enough to be certain in an uncertain world.

IDEALISM: Appreciate that your pains make up who you are and there is adventure in meeting life's challenges.

JUSTICE: Innocently recognise everyone has their own truth.

Here it is! Your Kitching Whittaker Enneagram Number!

YOUR NUMBER TYPE REVEALED

Here follows a summary of all the information you shall ever need about all the number types - plus a bit more. Do you know what to buy for your loved one's birthday that will REALLY make them happy?

There now follows a summary of qualities of being your particular number type. When you DISSOLVE, you dissolve to the WORST of the number you dissolve to. When you EVOLVE you evolve to the BEST of the number you evolve to. The Wings are where you lean to, being your neighbouring number types. Your polarity is what you are like at your very best and at your very worst!

Time to Be No.1

I strive to live the right way, to improve myself and others and avoid becoming angry. If I can make a difference in this world and make it a better place, then that truly is a life well lived. I am The Right One.

1: The Right One
SUMMARY: Conscientious and ethical with a strong sense of right and wrong.
Striving to improve and afraid of mistakes.
Orderly and fastidious.
Can be critical and perfectionistic.

POLARITY: Highly Principled to Self Righteous OCD
BEST: Discerning and wise, realistic and noble. Morally Heroic.
FEAR: Being corrupt/bad/evil.
DESIRE: To be good, to have integrity and to be balanced.
WINGS: +9=Idealist +2=Advocate

MOTIVATIONS: To be right. To improve everything and to be beyond criticism, so as not to be condemned by anyone.
DISSOLVING: 4=moody and irrational
EVOLVING: 7=joyful and spontaneous
TRIAD: GUT - Anger/Rage – Instinctive
REALITY: Holy Perfection
FIXATION: Resentment
AVOIDANCE: Anger
VIRTUE: Serenity
TRAP: Perfection

More, more more!
If you want to read more about the deeper concepts in the Kitching Whittaker Enneagram, **go to the Chapter entitled Going Deeper: The Beginnings of Distrust and Separation', PAGE 120**

If you wish to skip to the Typing Tunnel and double-check your number type, **go to the Chapter entitled 'Your Typing Tunnel', PAGE 142**

Or, if you are ready to discover your number's deeper meaning, then **go to the Chapter entitled 'The Hidden Secret at Your Core & 'The Way Forward', PAGE 275**

It's Time to Help You No.2s

I like for others to be happy. I like to be appreciated and to express my positive feelings to others so they feel good. I would do anything for you and I like to be liked. I am The Helpful One.

2: The Helpful One
SUMMARY: Empathetic, sincere and warmhearted. Friendly, generous and self-sacrificing. Sentimental, flattering and people pleasing. Driven to be close to others but need to be needed. Problems with possessiveness and acknowledging own needs.

POLARITY: Altruistic to Manipulative Martyr
BEST: Unselfish and altruistic with unconditional love for others.
FEAR: Of being unwanted, unworthy of love
DESIRE: To feel loved
WINGS: +1=The Servant +3=The Host

MOTIVATIONS: To express their feelings to others, to be appreciated and to get others to respond, to vindicate their claims about themselves.
DISSOLVING: 8=aggressive and dominating
EVOLVING: 4=self-nurturing and emotionally aware
TRIAD: HEART - Shame – Feeling
REALITY: Holy Will
AVOIDANCE: Neediness
VIRTUE: Humility
TRAP: Freedom

More, more more!
If you want to read more about the deeper concepts in the Kitching Whittaker Enneagram, **go to the Chapter entitled Going Deeper: The Beginnings of Distrust and Separation', PAGE 120**

If you wish to skip to the Typing Tunnel and double-check your number type**, go to the Chapter entitled 'Your Typing Tunnel', PAGE 142**

Or, if you are ready to discover your number's deeper meaning, then **go to the Chapter entitled 'The Hidden Secret at Your Core & 'The Way Forward', PAGE 275**

Time to Be Image Free for No.3s

I want to be productive, to succeed and to avoid failing. I am always working towards something and it's important I give out the right image. I am The Striving for Success One.

3: The Striving for Success One
SUMMARY: Self-assured, attractive and charming. Ambitious, competent and energetic. Can be status conscious and highly driven. Can be overly concerned with image and what others think. Workaholics and competitive.

POLARITY: Ambitious to Vindictive
BEST: Authentic role models who inspire others. Self accepting.
FEAR: Being worthless
DESIRE: To feel valuable and worthwhile
WINGS: +2=The Charmer +=The Professional

MOTIVATIONS: Distinguish oneself from others, to have attention, to impress.
DISSOLVING: 9=Apathy and disengaged
EVOLVING: 6=Co-operative and committed to others
TRIAD: HEART – Shame – Feeling
REALITY: Holy Law
FIXATION: Vanity
AVOIDANCE: Failure
VIRTUE: Veracity
TRAP: Efficiency

More, more more!
If you want to read more about the deeper concepts in the Kitching Whittaker Enneagram, **go to the Chapter entitled Going Deeper: The Beginnings of Distrust and Separation', PAGE 120**

If you wish to skip to the Typing Tunnel and double-check your number type**, go to the Chapter entitled 'Your Typing Tunnel', PAGE 142**

Or, if you are ready to discover your number's deeper meaning, then **go to the Chapter entitled 'The Hidden Secret at Your Core & 'The Way Forward', PAGE 275**

Time to Be More for All the 4s

I wonder about the true meaning of life, I appreciate beauty and seek it out. I want to understand my complex feelings, to be understood and to avoid being ordinary. I am The Only One.

4: The I'm the Only One
SUMMARY: Self aware, sensitive and reserved. Emotionally honest, creative and personal but can be moody and self conscious. Exempt from ordinary ways of living, having problems with melancholy and self pity.

POLARITY: Creative to Melancholy Self Contempt
BEST: Inspired and highly creative and able to renew themselves
FEAR: No identity or personal significance
DESIRE: To create identity for themselves, to find their significance

WINGS: +3=The Aristocrat +5=The Bohemian
MOTIVATIONS: Express themselves and their individuality, to create beauty, to maintain certain moods and feelings. To withdraw to protect self image. Take care of emotional needs before anything else. To attract a rescuer.
DISSOLVING: 2=Over involved and clingy
EVOLVING: 1=Objective and principled
TRIAD: HEART – Shame – Feeling
REALITY: Holy Origin
FIXATION: Melancholy
AVOIDANCE: Despair
VIRTUE: Equanimity
TRAP: Authenticity

More, more more!
If you want to read more about the deeper concepts in the Kitching Whittaker Enneagram, **go to the Chapter entitled Going Deeper: The Beginnings of Distrust and Separation', PAGE 120**

If you wish to skip to the Typing Tunnel and double-check your number type**, go to the Chapter entitled 'Your Typing Tunnel', PAGE 142**

Or, if you are ready to discover your number's deeper meaning, then **go to the Chapter entitled 'The Hidden Secret at Your Core & 'The Way Forward', PAGE 275**

Time to Thrive For No.5s

I enjoy my own company. I am self-sufficient and I strive to avoid looking foolish. I am always very interested in something. I am The Thoughtful One.

5: The Thoughtful One
SUMMARY: Alert and curious. Concentrate on complexity. Inventive but can be preoccupied with imaginary constructs. Detached, highly strung and intense, isolation.

POLARITY: Visionary to Obsessive Recluse
BEST: Visionary pioneer and innovator
FEAR: Being useless or incapable
DESIRE: To be capable and competent
WINGS: +4=Iconoclast +6=Problem Solver
MOTIVATIONS: To possess knowledge and understand environment. To have everything figured out; to defend self from threats.
DISSOLVING: 7=Hyperactive and scattered
EVOLVING: 8=Self confident and decisive

TRIAD: HEAD – Fear - Thinking
REALITY: Holy Omniscience
FIXATION: Stinginess
AVOIDANCE: Emptiness
VIRTUE: Non-attachment
TRAP: Observer

More, more more!
If you want to read more about the deeper concepts in the Kitching Whittaker Enneagram, **go to the Chapter entitled Going Deeper: The Beginnings of Distrust and Separation', PAGE 120**

If you wish to skip to the Typing Tunnel and double-check your number type, **go to the Chapter entitled 'Your Typing Tunnel', PAGE 142**

Or, if you are ready to discover your number's deeper meaning, then **go to the Chapter entitled 'The Hidden Secret at Your Core & 'The Way Forward', PAGE 275**

Time for The Unrestrictive No.6s

I like to know I can handle whatever situation comes up. I like to have your approval and enjoy supportive friends. I can be assertive or rebellious. I tend to question things a lot and prepare. I need to know I can trust you. I am The Safe One.

6: The Safe One
SUMMARY: Committed, security orientated. Reliable and hardworking. Responsible and trustworthy. Can be defensive and anxious. Cautious and indecisive reactive and rebellious.

POLARITY: Hardworking Stability to Paranoid Persecution
BEST: Stable and self reliant; courageously championing self and others
FEAR: Without support or guidance
DESIRE: To have security and support

WINGS: +5=Defender +7=Buddy
MOTIVATIONS: To reduce risks; security and support of others; to have reassurance, to test the attitudes of others towards them, fighting against insecurity.
DISSOLVING: 3=Competitive and arrogant
EVOLVING: 9=Relaxed and optimistic
TRIAD: HEAD – Fear – Thinking
REALITY: Holy Faith
FIXATION: Cowardice
AVOIDANCE: Deviance
VIRTUE: Courage
TRAP: Security

More, more more!
If you want to read more about the deeper concepts in the Kitching Whittaker Enneagram, **go to the Chapter entitled Going Deeper: The Beginnings of Distrust and Separation', PAGE 120**

If you wish to skip to the Typing Tunnel and double-check your number type**, go to the Chapter entitled 'Your Typing Tunnel', PAGE 142**

Or, if you are ready to discover your number's deeper meaning, then **go to the Chapter entitled 'The Hidden Secret at Your Core & 'The Way Forward', PAGE 275**

Time to Get Out Of Heaven, No.7s

I like to stay happy and positive and to keep on the go. I have a lot of projects happening. I am keen to explore possibilities. I keep away from restriction and pain and suffering. I am The Fun One.

7: The Fun One
SUMMARY: Extroverted, optimistic, versatile and spontaneous. Playful and high spirited and practical but can misapply talents, becoming scattered and undisciplined, exhausted.

POLARITY: Joyous to Materialistic Excess
BEST: Focussed on worthwhile goals; appreciative, joyous and satisfied
FEAR: Trapped and in pain
DESIRE: Satisfied and content
WINGS: +6=Entertainer +8=Realist

MOTIVATIONS: Maintain freedom and avoid missing out. Keeping preoccupied to avoid and discharge pain
DISSOLVING: 1=hugely critical
EVOLVING: 5=focused and fascinated
TRIAD: HEAD – Fear – Thinking
REALITY: Holy Plan
FIXATION: Planning
AVOIDANCE: Pain
VIRTUE: Sobriety
TRAP: Idealism

More, more more!
If you want to read more about the deeper concepts in the Kitching Whittaker Enneagram, **go to the Chapter entitled Going Deeper: The Beginnings of Distrust and Separation', PAGE 120**

If you wish to skip to the Typing Tunnel and double-check your number type, **go to the Chapter entitled 'Your Typing Tunnel', PAGE 142**

Or, if you are ready to discover your number's deeper meaning, then **go to the Chapter entitled 'The Hidden Secret at Your Core & 'The Way Forward', PAGE 275**

No Time To Infuriate the No.8s

> *I often end up in charge and I don't like it if I think anything or anyone is trying to control me. I can always rely upon myself and I avoid weakness. I can be very strong for you if I choose to protect you. I am The War One.*

8: The War One
SUMMARY: Self confident, strong and assertive. Protective and resourceful but can be egocentric and domineering.

POLARITY: Magnanimous to Vengeful
BEST: Self mastering, heroic and magnanimous
FEAR: Harmed or controlled by others
DESIRE: To be in control of life
WINGS: +7=Maverick +9=Bear
MOTIVATIONS: Self reliant to prove strength; to be important and dominate environment. To stay in control and set clear boundaries.

DISSOLVING: 5=secretive and fearful
EVOLVING: 2=optimistic and caring
TRIAD: GUT – Anger/Rage – Instinctive
REALITY: Holy Truth
FIXATION: Vengeance
AVOIDANCE: Weakness
VIRTUE: Innocence
TRAP: Justice

More, more more!
If you want to read more about the deeper concepts in the Kitching Whittaker Enneagram, **go to the Chapter entitled Going Deeper: The Beginnings of Distrust and Separation', PAGE 120**

If you wish to skip to the Typing Tunnel and double-check your number type**, go to the Chapter entitled 'Your Typing Tunnel', PAGE 142**

Or, if you are ready to discover your number's deeper meaning, then **go to the Chapter entitled 'The Hidden Secret at Your Core & 'The Way Forward', PAGE 275**

Time to Re-Align the No.9s

I like to connect personally with others and hate disagreements and matters of conflict, which I often try to resolve for others though not for myself. I am The Peace One.

9. The Peace One
SUMMARY: Accepting, trusting and stable. Creative, optimistic and supportive but can be too willing to go along with others to keep the peace.

POLARITY: Optimistic Unity to Dissociated Non-Function
BEST: Indomitable and all embracing, bring people together, healing conflicts
FEAR: Loss and separation
DESIRE: Inner stability and peace of mind
WINGS: +8=Referee +1=Dreamer

MOTIVATIONS: Create harmony and avoid conflicts in order to create inner calm.
DISSOLVING: 6=anxious and worried
EVOLVING: 3=self developing and energetic
TRIAD: GUT – Anger/Rage - Instinctive
REALITY: Holy Love
FIXATION: Indolence
AVOIDANCE: Conflict
VIRTUE: Action
TRAP: Seeker

More, more more!
If you want to read more about the deeper concepts in the Kitching Whittaker Enneagram, **go to the Chapter entitled Going Deeper: The Beginnings of Distrust and Separation', PAGE 120**

If you wish to skip to the Typing Tunnel and double-check your number type, **go to the Chapter entitled 'Your Typing Tunnel', PAGE 142**

Or, if you are ready to discover your number's deeper meaning, then **go to the Chapter entitled 'The Hidden Secret at Your Core & 'The Way Forward', PAGE 275**

Exclusive to Kitching Whittaker Enneagram

The Hidden Secret at Your Core & The Way Forward

In our experience as Practitioners we have found over the years that certain situations, illnesses and psychological issues tend to be attracted to specific Enneagram types.

In this final and unique section of the book we now explore some common issues for each of the Enneagram types, their structure and a way forward designed specifically for that Enneagram type.

The Way Forward for 1s

----Anything less than accepting imperfection in the world isn't avoiding anger isn't it? ----

Predisposition: Obsessive Compulsive Disorder (OCD) and Anger

The Type 1's ultimate goal is perfection in everything that they do.

In the extreme this can lead to OCD.

Being obsessed about *getting things done right* might not sound like a problem, but this focus is masking a deeper issue.

The Type 1 wants to be *perfect in mind, body and soul*.

This is of course impossible.

So why has Type 1 created an impossible task and dedicated their life to it: what is the Type 1 secret?

What is the secret behind the smoke & mirrors?

It is this: the Type 1 does not want to acknowledge the bad, corrupt or flawed part of themselves.

We all have these things within us, but the 1 feels that they will never progress as a human being unless they can smother this dark part of their soul.

But the Type 1 must face this truth, because in order to achieve their ultimate goal of serenity, like yin and yang they must *accept that they have good and bad within themselves thereby achieve balance*. Once this happens any anger issues or OCD will begin to fade.

----Anything less than enjoying my imperfect self isn't serenity isn't it? ----

The Way Forward for 2s

----Anything less than helping in moderation isn't being wanted and loved isn't it? ----

Predisposition: Not Being Able to Say No and Exhaustion / Burnout

Type 2 *loves to help* because it gives them a sense of being wanted and loved.

In moderation this is fine, but when Type 2 go too far they become a martyr. At the extreme they can become possessive and manipulative.

Type 2 feel that by looking after everyone else they will achieve freedom from their needs and find humility.

This is of course impossible.

Freedom from looking after oneself or your own needs can never be achieved so they spiral into exhaustion helping many people or become overly possessive and manipulative, believing they are indispensable to a closely guarded few.

So why has Type 2 created an impossible task and dedicated their life to it, what is the Type 2 secret?

What is the secret behind the smoke & mirrors?

The 2 does not want to face the fact that they have needs because this is selfish and will stop them achieving humility.

The key to moving forward for the 2 is to accept that *there is no shame in having needs* and that sometimes the 2 will need to fulfil those needs themselves.

The other important journey for the 2 is that *true love can only come from within not without*.

----Anything less than accepting my own love and help isn't humility isn't it? ----

The Way Forward for 3s

----Anything less than accepting oneself isn't feeling valuable and worthwhile isn't it? ----

Predisposition: Burnout and Drug Addiction

Without achievement the 3 does not exist.

Efficiency, *hard work and pursuing ever greater achievements* is the aim of the Type 3 in order to achieve the ultimate goal of being valued and deemed worthy by all.

This is of course impossible.

As the achievements are a never ending cascade of bigger houses, or faster cars, or the latest designer labels, or the next promotion, there always seems to be something new to achieve for the 3s?

So why has Type 3 created an impossible task and dedicated their life to it, what is the Type 3 secret?

What is the secret behind the smoke & mirrors?

The 3 is in fact *running from their own existence*.

By accepting that they exist as a worthwhile human being as they are right now, they can stop the never ending struggle to fulfil their ever inflating *image of success*.

----Anything less than accepting my worth as I am right now isn't being someone isn't it? ----

The Way Forward for 4s

----Anything less than accepting the ordinary isn't being authentic isn't it? ----

Predisposition: Mystery Illness

If a 4 takes a significant blow to what they perceive as being their identity, such as their chosen career in which they excel has been taken from them, or they are suddenly removed without choice from their home or home town in which they feel they have stamped their identity, the 4 will react.

This reaction is based on a loss of *significance which they feel is their identity*.

The 4 may attempt to quickly regain significance / identity by developing a unique or rare mystery illness.

It will be virtually impossible for medical professionals to diagnose the issue no matter how many tests they run and, to the anger of the 4, medical professionals will often say that their symptoms are impossible.

On a subconscious level the 4 attempts to gain

personal significance / identity from a unique illness.

This is of course impossible.

The 4 is simply branded as one of the many hypochondriacs or attention seekers in the world which certainly does not give them the significance / identity that they were searching for.

So why does the Type 4 attempt to regain identity this way, what is the Type 4 secret?

What is the secret behind the smoke & mirrors?

The 4 refuses to accept that they are like everyone else. If there is any *danger of them becoming a part of the norm they feel that they will simply disappear.*

The way forward for the 4 is to accept that *they have personal significance just by being alive* as the person that they are right now. If they can achieve this, then many of their issues would simply fade away.

----Anything less than accepting my significance as I am right now isn't equilibrium isn't it? ----

The Way Forward for 5s

----Anything less than accepting the unknown isn't self assuredness isn't it? ----

Predisposition: Anxiety, Depression and Over Thinking

The world of the 5 is a never ending *search for information in order to know the unknown.*

The 5 is always on the lookout for more information on their environment so they can allay unknown fears and all negative eventualities.

This is of course impossible.

So why has Type 5 created an impossible task and dedicated their life to it, what is the Type 5 secret?

What is the secret behind the smoke & mirrors?

The 5 refuses to accept the unknown because it may find them useless or incompetent. By attaining knowledge they can vanquish their inadequacies. The way forward is to accept that *not knowing can be just as empowering as knowing*.
Once accepted, their anxiety and depression will

simply fade away.

----Anything less than knowing that I don't have to know, isn't peace of mind isn't it?----

The Way Forward for 6s

----Anything less than accepting insecurity in the world isn't certainty isn't it? ----

Predisposition: Fibromyalgia (Fibro)

The structure of the Type 6 reality is based on support and security.

The Type 6 will *give their all to a relationship or job that they think is bringing support and security into their reality*.

If, for whatever reason, this security is suddenly withdrawn or threatened through divorce or an adverse change at work, the Type 6 will feel betrayed and will react quickly in an attempt to fill the security vacuum that has been left behind.

The size of the reaction will depend on the size of the vacuum. *In an extreme case an illness such as Fibromyalgia may develop* in order to bring support and security.

The Fibro paradox: at first glance the debilitating symptoms of Fibro appear to be the opposite of what the Type 6 wants, support and security.

However, when you look at the ecology of Fibro we start to see a different picture.

In the western world many Governments are recognising Fibro as a legitimate illness (which it is) and are building support and security networks for sufferers.

Friends and family members tend to rally around and give support and security to a family member who has Fibro. The debilitating symptoms themselves often leave sufferers with no energy and they must spend a day or days in bed to recover. On a conceptual level your bed offers the ultimate in support and security.

The 6 journey is a search for someone or something that will give them *financial and emotional support, plus security and will never let them down*.

This is of course impossible.

So why has Type 6 created an impossible task and dedicated their life to it, what is the Type 6 secret?

What is the secret behind the smoke & mirrors?

The 6 feels that as long as they have support and security behind them, they have the courage to achieve anything.

So, how does a Type 6 escape Fibro? The fastest way to escape is to develop a support and security structure in something other than illness, such as a relationship, career, vocation, hobby or anything that has a support network built into it and some form of security.

It will be hard at first for the Type 6 to breakaway from Fibro and the symptoms will attack with vengeance but this will be a sign and a signal that the Type 6 is on the right track.

The 6 can then take the next step which is *acknowledging that their own inner resources will give them strength and courage to achieve anything.*

----Anything less than self reliance isn't courage isn't it? ----

The Way Forward for 7s

----Anything less than accepting that life isn't ideal isn't avoiding pain isn't it? ----

Predisposition: Depression

When the Type 7's reality comes crashing in and the possibility of their fantasy world becomes impossible, a 7 may experience depression.

The 7 is always looking to move from pain and is in a constant search for *the ideal career, job, house, partner etc*.

This is of course impossible.

So why has Type 7 created an impossible task and dedicated their life to it, what is the Type 7 secret?

What is the secret behind the smoke & mirrors?

The 7 does not want to admit to themselves that *they are currently in pain*.

By constantly running from past emotional pain they are *trapped forever within it whenever it comes to mind*.

The way forward for the 7 is to acknowledge their pain, feel it and release it and then they can stop searching for the ultimate ideal and truly see the reality that is around them, which of course includes pleasure and pain. They could then *use their creativity to create a realistic ideal that is sustainable*.

----Anything less than me fully experiencing both pleasure and pain isn't being free isn't it? ----

The Way Forward for 8s

----Anything less than relinquishing control of life isn't strength isn't it? ----

Predisposition: Food Control Issues

The 8 will typically have a fraught relationship with food, because this is the first point in their lives when they experience being controlled.

As a child, parents decide what time you eat, where you eat and what you eat. This is often a hidden trauma / injustice for the 8 that they never really recover from (8s can sometimes have sleep issues also because parents also controlled their sleep and wake up times).

In adult life the 8 may tend to hoard and or binge eat food as a subconscious *act of defiance against the injustice* of the parents' or carers' past food control.

However they then feel controlled by the food and they will attempt to regain control by over exercise to burn off the calories or by medical intervention such as gastric band surgery.

In extreme situations they may use Bulimia or Anorexia as a tool to gain total control.

Ultimately, the 8 world is one of vengeance in order to right the past injustice and gain ultimate control so as to never be controlled ever again.

This is of course impossible.

So why has Type 8 created an impossible task and dedicated their life to it, what is the Type 8 secret?

What is the secret behind the smoke & mirrors?

The 8 does not want to admit that they are currently being controlled. Deep down they feel that bodily functions such as hunger, thirst, tiredness, etc are controlling them but they refuse to face this.

The ultimate feeling of loss of control for the 8 is of course life. Many 8's are strong proponents of euthanasia so they can feel a sense of control over the ultimate unknown.

The way forward for the 8 is to admit and accept that *they are being controlled on a daily basis but that not all control is malevolent* and is in fact just a part of the everyday flow of life. Once they take this journey their food issues will soon fade away.

----Anything less than my not searching for justice isn't finding innocence isn't it? ----

The Way Forward for 9s

----Anything less than not seeking harmony isn't avoiding conflict isn't it? ----

Predisposition: Dependant Personality Disorder and Lack of Self Care

The 9 world is one of *searching for and creating harmony at all costs*.

Unfortunately, the cost is almost always borne by the 9.

For a 9 it has become selfish to think about the self and selfishness is the ultimate crime for the 9.

Their aim is to create harmony for all by absorbing all of the negativity and conflict in their environment.

This is of course impossible.

So why has Type 9 created an impossible task and dedicated their life to it, what is the Type 9 secret?

What is the secret behind the smoke & mirrors?

The 9 is chasing harmony at their expense so they can avoid loss and separation which is their biggest fear.

Deep down inside the 9 has *lost and been separated from their own needs and desires* for some time. The way forward for the 9 is to reunite with their own desires and needs. The next step is to then accept that *losing and being separated from negative individuals in their life is fantastic and something to be celebrated!*

----Anything less than my accepting loss and separation isn't taking harmonising action isn't it? ---

Fame and Fortune Typed!
-Donald Trump

The Evidence

*It has been reported that Trump's father was a workaholic, a strict disciplinarian and was also 'tight-fisted'. He was determined to toughen up his sons. This parental behavioural pattern is consistent with an 8 childhood.

*Reports say that throughout Donald's life he would never admit that he was wrong, no matter how trivial the subject.
This is consistent with an 8.

*Trump openly admits he was a trouble maker as a youngster and is still so today, commenting, 'I like to stir things up and I like to test people'.
Wanting to test people (some might say bully) is classic 8 behaviour.

*He also said, 'it wasn't malicious so much as it was aggressive.'
The fact that he is comfortable with being aggressive also fits an 8 behaviour pattern.

It has been argued that Donald Trump is a 3, showing signs of entrepreneurial behavior and seemingly obsessed with image however in light of the above evidence we believe that his interest in image is purely a tool that he uses to control others. The Kitching Whittaker Enneagram .

In Book 2 of the Kitching Whittaker Enneagram we will typing more famous / infamous people.
Send us an email and let us know who you would like typed.
Send suggestions to: **info@hiprocom.com** with "Famous Type" in the subject area.

Countries of the World Typed!

-Greece

The Evidence

They are typically a passionate people. In our experience Greek nationals are avid helpers and very sociable people. They like being different from the norm and are proud of their identity and national themes.
This would put Greece in the Heart triad and a strong identity is indicative of a type 4.

Greek people are often very nostalgic about how good things used to be. The music often reflects a melancholic respect for days gone by. The term Greek Tragedy is of course part of common parlance. Sometimes true stories are relayed with a measure of dramatic influence.

Melancholy is a classic 4 trait.

Nationals have a very strong and proud identity which is displayed in their distinctive food and their unabashed Greek dancing when the spirit moves them.

Men, women and children of all ages revel in the freedom and technique of spontaneous displays of the Sirtaki, for example. This identity travels with them wherever they happen to find themselves in the world.

A strong sense of identity and artistic / creative leanings (dance) is indicative of type 4.

There is still a great deal of superstition around in Greece. The 'Evil Eye' is a talisman that adorns many homes and shops in Greece.

.

Type 4 is often drawn towards fantasy, surreal and the darker side of life.

The Greek people, generally speaking, tend to react in an emotionally charged manner to frustration. This is a classic type 4 behavioural pattern.

From our analysis Greece is type 4.

In book 2 of the Kitching Whittaker Enneagram we will typing more countries.

Send us an email and let us which country you would like typed.
Send suggestions to: **info@hiprocom.com** with "Country Type" in the subject area.

Coming Soon!
BOOK 2 of The Kitching Whittaker Enneagram Adventure

*Find your perfect partner or improve your current relationship.

*Find the right career for your personality type.

*Find the best parenting strategy for child's type.

*Find the answer to your social, home and work issues.

*And more celebrity and country typing!

Tell us about your issue

For each of the above sections we are looking for real life issues to solve using the Enneagram.

Email your issue to: **info@hiprocom.com** with "real life example" in the subject area.

If we use your issue in the next book all names will be changed to protect your identity.

Thank you for reading
The Kitching Whittaker Enneagram Adventure!

Please leave a review on Amazon and let us know what you thought.

Your review is very important to us.

Contact us at info@hiprocom.com.

Other titles available:
Diploma in Clinical Hypnotherapy & NLP
Advanced Diploma in Hypnotherapy
Panic Stations Guide To Deception Analysis
Panic Stations Guide To Statement Analysis
Fifty Simplified Quantum Physics Facts
The Twelve Trials of the Law of Attraction
Speak Greek Badly in 20 Min
Easy UK Law